Love Makes Life

Rev. Arthur H. DeKruyter

 Tyndale House Publishers, Inc. Wheaton, Illinois

Unless otherwise noted, all Scripture references
are from the King James Version of the Bible.
Other references are from the *Revised
Standard Version* (RSV), Copyright © 1952 by
the Division of Christian Education of the
National Council of Churches of Christ in the
United States of America, and *The Living Bible*
(TLB), Copyright © 1971 by Tyndale House
Publishers.

First printing, September 1981

Library of Congress Catalog Card Number 81-51322
ISBN 0-8423-3849-7 paper
Copyright © 1981 by Arthur H. DeKruyter
All rights reserved
Printed in the United States of America

Contents

Preface

Some of our experiences, though uncomfortable, are inherent in the process of living. We do not choose them. But we cannot avoid them. They upset our quest for happiness. They interrupt our plans for peace and security. They threaten our very existence. They lead us to ask if these painful experiences have a higher purpose.

Other experiences have the potential for great happiness and fulfillment or great agony and misery. The basic relationships of marriage and the family can be among the most productive or the most destructive. Our understanding, expectation, and attitudes about human relationships often make the difference between years of enjoyment or of frustration.

To assume that there must be a higher purpose for the experiences of life prompts a variety of questions. Is it possible that many of these relationships are archaic and outmoded? Some very articulate and popular thought leaders propose that the basic structures of life ought to change. They propose that deliberate action be taken to destroy some of these most sacred institutions in order to obviate the miseries of life which often accompany them.

In this book I have asked some of the difficult but necessary questions about our experiences and relationships to determine whether or not we can find purpose in our structures and institutions. I strongly believe we are missing the ways of enrichment which the Creator has for us because we do not understand his methods of dealing with our lives.

In this book we will deal with aspects of human relationships which are common to all of us. They puzzle us because of the changing attitudes about them and the conflicting opinions of the experts.

I want to probe the Christian mind and propose the alternative of biblical thought to such experiences as suffering, loneliness, grief, and death. Before we discard our historical values and practices of marriage and the home, I want to see a higher ideal for the family, parents, and sex.

I am convinced that God has a noble purpose for the relationships he sometimes gives us in marriage and the family and which he sometimes allows to be taken from us through suffering, separation, divorce, and death. In all of these changing relationships, God can teach us more about ourselves, and, most important, about our eternal relationship with him.

Relationships We Build

Husband-wife and parent-child relationships, from which we derive so much meaning and purpose in life, become what we make them to be. They begin as legal and physical union and sometimes remain no more than that. Because of sin in the world and human nature, we only glimpse what these human relationships could and should be. But even our fleeting glimpses and efforts at accomplishing the ideal are enough to show us what these unions were intended to provide — a mirror of our relationship to God as heavenly Bridegroom and heavenly Father.

If these most meaningful relationships are to grow and accomplish God's purpose in the world, they require our most positive and constructive efforts. When we see God's purpose in these unions, we understand their emphasis in the Scriptures and, more important, why God is so concerned to help us make these relationships all they ought to be.

When Two Are One

Marriage can succeed because our Creator has purposed it to succeed. Because so many marriages are in trouble does not mean that getting married is not wise. The current crises merely indicate that we are straying a long way from the original design. Sometimes we tinker so much with a product that we destroy its usefulness. In the case of marriage we need to recover the original blueprint.

Who was the architect of marriage? How did it originate? What was the purpose? The answers to these questions are found in both the Old and New Testaments. Jesus quoted the Old Testament when he said, "What therefore God hath joined together let not man put asunder" (Matt. 19:6).

The occasion to which he referred took place in the Garden of Eden. When God had created all things and had finally created a man, he said that his creation was still incomplete because man was alone. Even though the first man could talk to God and was the ruler over all of the garden and the animals, he had no one with whom he could share his life. "It is not good that man should be alone," God said. It is still not good to be alone.

Loneliness is one of our major concerns today. We have so few true friends upon whom we can rely. Even sacred covenants and commitments, which are intended to last a lifetime, sometimes fail. Relationships today are usually conditional and often expire at the first indication of crisis. If we don't achieve the self-gratification we sought, we become expert at finding reasons to terminate our involvements with those whom we thought would bring us happiness.

God's answer to the need of the first lonely man was marriage. He created a woman, brought her to the man, and enjoined them to live in harmony together. In God's creative wisdom, he designed that man and woman would complement each other with such beauty that their union reflected his own image.

And the man and the woman became "one flesh." That expression has very strong meaning—far more than just physical relationship. It means that their lives became enmeshed, interwoven; they became one, and in that oneness they found completeness, wholeness, and the answer to the deep need for companionship. In reflecting upon that concept, Paul wrote in 1 Corinthians 11 that as man and woman were created separately and distinctly with far deeper implications than just physical differences, so there is an order but yet an equality. In the mind of the Creator, they were given the dignity of his image, the ability to fellowship with him, and with him to purify and sanctify their own relationships.

A statement in Genesis is again quoted in the New Testament by Jesus: "For this reason a man shall leave his father and his mother." This means that the husband and wife relationship supersedes previous relationships. No one, particularly those who follow God's will, should ever intrude or in any way foster division or create polarization between a husband and a wife. That prohibition includes father and mother. No parent should ever indulge his or her child in order to satisfy some personal desire once the marriage has taken place. There should be parental support, but no married young person should hasten back home to get advice on how to handle problems which ought to be settled with his or her spouse. Marriage is a holy relationship, and woe to the person who intrudes, divides, or contributes to its dissolution. For "what . . . God hath joined together, let not man put asunder."

Man started with an ideal relationship, which became very dear to him. It was given as the illustration of God's relationship to his people, reflecting the covenantal bond which he established with Abraham when he said, "I will establish my covenant between me and thee and thy seed after thee in their generations for an everlasting covenant, to be a God unto thee, and to thy seed after thee" (Gen. 17:7). God called himself the husband of his loving bride, Israel. One of the prophets, Hosea, became an example of that marriage. Hosea pursued his wife who had betrayed him by prostituting herself. She was finally auctioned off at the slave market. And like God, Hosea pursued his much-loved wife, Gomer, retrieved her, and redeemed her—bought her back—as his own in spite of the blighted life she had lived. Such, we read in the Scriptures, is an illustration of the love and the pursuing grace of God. In the New Testament it is the same kind of love that Christ has for his Church. Marriage became a symbol of how God and his people love each other, sacrifice for one another, respond to each other.

In Scripture we read, "Husbands, love your wives as Christ loved the Church." This lays upon the man a greater responsibility of grace and of sacrifice, a more weighty leadership within marriage, something to be assumed with an attitude of awe. One must continue to pursue and pursue, even as God in the Old Testament pursued his people, and as Jesus in the New Testament gave his life to redeem those who did not even want him. That is the high goal God established for marriage.

Paul said there were two things that Jesus did for the Church that husbands must do for their wives. They must give themselves, and they must make them holy. Peter wrote that a husband needs to see to the fulfillment of his wife (1 Peter 3:7). It is a heavy responsibility. The husband is to be the spiritual leader in the marriage. He is the initiator; he establishes the basis for values. He must bring to his marriage a quality of life that will establish once and for all a solid foundation.

And the wife is to be responsive to that love. As the Church and as believing Christians, she must out of gratitude be responsive to all the goodness that is offered her. Scripture says that she is to be a helpmeet, supporting and completing, making the totality a well-founded one. She was the one who brought meaning to the lonely man in Eden.

God established all this before sin entered the world. There were no problems in the garden when the woman was brought to the man. The husband-wife relationship became a paradigm for all the relationships that God willed for mankind—the relationships of trust, of true friendship, of solid lifetime commitments on which people could depend. What could be more beautiful! God offered all this when he instituted marriage.

From this we should find some practical meaning which will help us in our marriages. It would be easy for me just to state rules about how to have a good marriage. We are rapidly becoming a nation of rules. We think that if we could pass enough laws in our country, we could govern all the activities of mankind. We could say, "If you do this and that, you will have a successful marriage." But that is not the way life is lived. We will never have a successful and strong nation by legislation alone. We will never build strong marriages that way. The letter of the law does not build strong marriages; the spirit of the law does. Life amounts to more than keeping data and taking surveys. Life is lived through relationships that are rooted in the heart. Christ came to change hearts, not to change laws. Jesus fulfilled, defined, and extended law but never negated it. At the same time, he came to give us new attitudes, new interests, new aspirations, new hopes, new desires. We press on because of what we see in our mind's eye and because of the goals and ideals of God Almighty. He gives us this picture of marriage, and now we struggle to fulfill it—each one of us in his own way, complicated by all kinds of problems but supported by the Spirit which gives life and renewal to us.

For a Christian, the first important truth about marriage is to recognize the realism of it. It is a very real thing to be a Christian. Sometimes when I read contemporary ideas about marriage, I scratch my head and say, "Who could believe that? It is utterly unrelated to reality. It not only does not work, but it never has worked and has no factual basis." Here in the Scripture we have God's definitions of marriage. He recognizes our problem of ideals in this world of hard reality. Nothing is ideal in this world, which is why Jesus came. He came because our marriages are not ideal. The reason is that *we* are not perfect. There is no way to make a perfect marriage with two imperfect people. We Christians forget this fact. We think that somehow there is something wrong with us when there are problems in our marriage. But marriage problems are not exceptional at all. They prove that we are human.

The Christian gospel means that human beings with problems in life can do something about them. We can admit them freely and

deal with them. We should not look for utopia in marriage. We are
realistic enough to know that we married a real human being,
and that a human being is married to us. When the two of us come
together, there are bound to be some areas of conflict.

And so we rejoice, in the first place because, although we have
that lofty, high ideal of marriage, we can be honest enough to
face the truth about how we live and what our lives are all about.
We can bring our differences openly to one another. That is part
of marriage. How honest are we with our marriage partners? Do
we ever tell our partners what we tell God about ourselves? Or,
do we try to act like we know what it is all about, and that it is our
partners who really do not? When we are a good friend, we
unmask ourselves. We talk to our partners about our problems,
and we admit them as we do to God. That is all part of being
married.

Forgiveness is a Christian virtue. Reconciliation is the
underlying meaning of that word. In forgiveness we bring together
that which has been separated and alienated. It means we try
again to focus on what is good. The power the Christian enjoys is
that healing which the Holy Spirit brings into marriage.

Realism is an essential ingredient. We face marital problems in
trust and with healing power. Jesus is within us to heal and to
bring us together, which is what he came to do.

Among all of the virtues of marriage is the basic quality of
love. The Christian dimension of love is different from the world's
understanding. If any of us were asked, "What is the greatest
thing we could do to keep our marriage together?" we would reply
that it is to show in some way our love to our partner every day.
That is a noble goal. But there is another dimension to the
Christian aspect of love as a healing power that we can have as a
Christian. We might ask ourselves, "How can I not only show my
love to my partner every day, but how can I show Christ's love to
my partner every day?" That is different. That dimension of love
gets to the heart of the person. It relates the whole attitude and
relationship of marriage to a far higher Being who came into a
troubled world to cleanse and redeem us.

Paul wrote, "Above all, put on love which binds everything
together in perfect harmony" (Col. 3:14, RSV). Though you
speak in your home and to your spouse with tongues of men and
angels, though you write beautiful sonnets and recite lovely

poetry, if you have not love, you are clanging brass. You are a cymbal, sounding with hollowness. Love makes the marriage successful. How do you show Christ's love to your spouse?

I invite you to consider what God wants you to be in your marriage. And if you plan to be married or are choosing a spouse, think about these truths with great care. Think of the heavy weight that is placed on the man in all that Scripture says, and of all the responsiveness that love provokes in a woman. Think how God will bless as he forgives and heals and renews daily. What a successful marriage that would make! All that God touches with his Spirit succeeds.

Christian marriage initiates relationships that excite the imagination and provide the basis of a strong and enriched society. Our nation and our institutions depend on our homes. The wealth of wisdom in the Scriptures will help us to understand the potential of family life and will give practical guidance for our conduct.

Specific relationships are established within the covenant of marriage. God's purpose extends to our responsibilities as spouses, parents, and homebuilders, relationships we will examine in subsequent chapters.

Family—The Home Base

When Orwell wrote his book, *1984*, he predicted that the family would be almost useless by the time the eighties arrived. Others reinforced his opinion, and some of them literally proposed that the family be abolished as an institution.

The family remains under severe attack. A British physician in his book, *The Death of the Family*, wrote that the family is the product of imperialism — in fact, a tool for imperialistic control. Kate Millet in her book, *Sexual Politics* (New York: Avon, 1971), claims that the family as an institution has been strong only in order to exploit women; and, therefore, it should be abolished. We are told that if we are to be free, we must be freed from the shackles of the family which is part of a past, no longer important, that is hampering our progress.

Today, happily, there can be found a more refreshing viewpoint. Michael Novak's column in the *Chicago Tribune* recently reminded us that 77 percent of our 214 million people in America are living in two-parent homes. Another 10 percent are living in homes where there is one parent. This means that 87 percent of our population is living in family relationships. The other 13 percent are those who have taken vows of celibacy, the widows and widowers, those in nursing homes, those living in communes, and the younger singles. But, as he points out, the media, probably looking for something either new or different, gives a totally wrong impression of what has been happening to the family. The family has not disappeared. It is very much alive in this country. And we cannot always trust those who bring us conflicting data as we seek to establish the generality or the norm.

We are encouraged particularly when such large secular organizations as the World Health Organization tell us that the family is sorely needed. It is in the family that the basic character traits of the individual are cultivated and developed. In the family one finds his or her stability for later life. It is because of broken families that we find so many broken lives today. We must repair the family.

The family is God's gift to us, not only reinforced by those who have evaluated and discovered its value, but reinforced by God himself. In Genesis 1 we see that God created all things. He created a man and said, "That is not enough. I need to finish what I have started." So he created also a woman, brought the two together, and established the family. Then he said, "That is very good." He was finished; he had completed his creative work.

The family became the unit in which children were to grow and develop in the context of love. It was the context in which they were to understand what life is all about, and who God is. The goal of parenting is to produce a mature child who, in young adulthood, has enough maturity to stand shoulder to shoulder as a peer with his parents in love for God, in purpose for life, and in respect for his fellow man. While the child is to honor parents always, he is to be treated as a brother or a sister in the context of God's kingdom. The ultimate blessing of family life will take place when we all assemble one day in the kingdom of God and fulfill what Jesus said when he reminded us: "Do not call anyone on earth 'father,' for you have one Father and he is in heaven" (Matt. 23:9, NIV). That is the goal of the family, and that is the fulfillment of biblical parenting. Children are indeed a heritage from the Lord. How wonderful for a child to be looked upon as a gift of God!

God's plan was that every child should have a good father and a good mother. Every child should have a home of good will and good humor, a home soundly based upon his Word and will. A home is where one can come with his successes to rejoice and his failures to be encouraged. Home is a place to escape from despair, to draw upon the wisdom of the more mature, a place to learn how to view immediate circumstances and how to see the more distant visions of life. It is a place where one can weep and laugh, a place where one can understand his greatest and deepest commitments. This is the ideal home. In that context God planned that the family was to be nurtured.

Beginning with the first book of the Bible, God recognized the family as the basic unit of society. He dealt not with individuals but primarily with family units. He called Abraham, the father of Israel, out of a city in Mesopotamia named Ur. He told Abraham and his children as a family unit that they would become a blessing to all the nations of the earth. God gave the sign of circumcision to be administered the eighth day after birth to the male members of his family. It was in the context of family that God was going to fulfill his promises to mankind, not to Abraham as an individual. And so God honored the family. Abraham had a son, Isaac, who had a son, Jacob, who had twelve sons who became the fathers of Israel. There were twelve tribes — really one great family. It is in that context that we understand worship in the Old Testament.

In Deuteronomy 6, we discover that it was the fathers who were told to talk to and teach their sons and daughters their spiritual heritage. And the knowledge of God was carried on from generation to generation by oral tradition through the family. The system known as Covenant Theology grew up around the concept of the family in the Old Testament carrying right through to the New Testament. In Matthew and Luke these genealogies of Jesus relate him to the family. Jesus came as a son of the family of David, of the family of Abraham. That is the way God meant it to be.

It is very significant that in our time, when the family is threatened, almost every school of biblical thought is turning to the Old Testament to reassess what God has done with the family. These scholars are all concluding that the family is one of the most significant factors in all of history.

We must remind ourselves that children are the heritage of the Lord, and the family is his gift. Whenever we see this belief contradicted, there is disaster. Caesar's wife, Claudia, exploited the family, killing off all those who would compete for their throne. Herod the Great practiced the same thing. Even among the leaders of Israel there was fratricide to gain the throne. Whenever there was division in the family, there was disaster. Jesus said, "Every . . . house divided against itself shall not stand" (Matt. 12:25). It is true today. Where there is conflict in the family — dissension,

disagreement— there is no security or stability for the children.
God has laid down the ground rules, and we cannot break them with
impunity.

The family is where we learn. Family life teaches us how to learn.
Many of us have read in years past that the first seven years of life
are the most important. More recently Dr. K. Couzman, whose
Ph.D. dissertation from UCLA was in child care, concluded that the
first three years of a child's life are the most significant. Dr.
Couzman claims that a child is trained in decision making, such
as deciding which toy to pick up in a playpen, how to live with
what he has decided upon, and some values, all by the example
of parents.

Dr. James Fowler, of Emory University, came to the same
conclusions, showing that decision making is not learned quite as
late in life as we may have thought. The learning process begins
while a child is being carried by its mother before birth. The whole
atmosphere and emotional quality, important for the future of
the family, develops throughout infancy and early childhood.

But other periods in life are important also. "A most critical
time," says Dr. Uris Bronfenbrenner of Cornell University, "is the
junior high years." He believes there is what he calls "inutility"
at that age. By that he means that a junior high student is
non-productive in our society, and yet he has the qualities and
characteristics of someone who could be productive. Junior high
students are young adults, maturing sexually, maturing
conceptually, playing with drugs and sex, experimenting at an age
when mother feels she does not have to be around while they
are at home. They can take care of themselves. Yet they cannot work
because child labor laws do not permit it. And so they do
nothing at that age in life that is really satisfying and productive.
They are the recipients of gifts and indulgence. They have
energy to burn. They must be doing something. And yet it is the
same time when, basically, they are ignored. Dr. Bronfenbrenner
says, "Competent, able, compassionate kids get turned into kids
out of *Lord of the Flies*," and I think he may be right. We ought
to pay more attention to some of these very difficult years of
adjustment. We ought to be training and developing not only
competency but responsibility and accountability as well—things
that will carry them through life.

We think our children are adults all at once when they reach high school. There has been a gap between the time they were little children and young adults. A survey was taken of three hundred junior high boys in grades seven and eight. The boys kept a log for two weeks to record how much time they spent each day with their fathers. It was discovered that most boys saw their fathers only at meals. Some of them did not see him from one week to the other. And the average that a boy saw his father, according to this survey, was seven and a half minutes per day. For those formative junior high years, this clearly is not enough. Dr. Bronfenbrenner says, "If we pay as much attention to the family as we do to firearms and football, this country would be a lot healthier and a lot happier."

Our families can be built up if someone in the family will just start. One person, catching a vision of what the family could be, thinking about the ideal, and then deciding to do something about it, can bring a healthy change. We need not tell anybody. We don't have to announce we are going to do something. We simply change our pattern. We begin to love and to be concerned.

One twenty-year-old son decided to do something about his family. He went up to his dad and said, "You know, Dad, you are really a neat guy."

His dad was rather startled and answered, "Well, Son, I think you are a pretty nice boy. In fact, I've been praying about our family situation for years." Suddenly they began to talk, and the whole family was turned around.

It does not necessarily take a parent to begin it. If there is too much tension and too much division, any one of the family can do something. Without announcing the plan, one simply begins to pray and to work to guide his own conduct in new ways so that the family can be rescued.

Another entirely different approach to doing something about the family was suggested in an article written by Fran Tarkenton, former quarterback of the Minnesota Vikings. Someone said to him, "Isn't it dull getting out of football and going into the business world?"

"Oh, no," he replied. "I don't think so at all. You know, football has its ups and downs. Much of the year there is nothing going on, and that part of the year isn't the greatest. That's not real life. That is just a game. Now I am in real life."

Since he left football, Tarkenton is consulting with executives and trying to repair the relationships of executives within their organizations. Businessmen often call members of their organizations together to talk about what ought to happen in the company. Concerned about the family, Tarkenton added, "You know what ought to happen? Executives ought to apply their creative know-how to their families." But they haven't been doing it.

It is not always people with authority who have ideas. It is people from the shop and people on the assembly line. Management gets all kinds of input. It is a new collegial world we are living in and everyone shares. Why do they not try it at home? Families have a lot of discretionary money, time, and vacation. Suppose the whole family came together and said, "We have some money and vacation time to spend. What shall we do with it?" instead of the parent saying "This is what we will do with it." We cannot do this in business anymore, and we should not do it in our families.

Tarkenton says great things are happening among executives who practice this. Executives also know the need for reinforcement. Of course a manager expects people to do their work. That is why he hires them. But he knows he has to pause and say to them, "You are doing a great job." When do we ever say that in the family? We use many creative ideas in management. How could a child learn any better than from his father as to why and how he lays away for his retirement years, or plans protection for the possibility of his wife becoming a widow? Responsibility and creativity—these are things that children can learn first-hand. And it can also be done in spiritual development.

I know one executive who made his family accountable to each other for a creative spiritual goal. At regular intervals, they came together, exchanged their goal ideas, and reported on progress or new goals. Conferences were not haphazard but regular. It gave his young children the idea that they ought to be thinking creatively not only in vocational, financial, and other matters, but also in spiritual matters.

There are some general things we can do for our families. But specifically we could install in our families to make them truly Christian something that might be called a security system. How do parents give a child, God's child, a sense of security on earth? There is no better way than to let the child see that parents are secure—mother and father, love flowing between them. Each should give a little word on the side once in a while about what a great dad they have or what a wonderful mother they have. Tell them you would not trade your partner for anybody in the world. They will know if you mean it and will be able to come to either parent in confidence. Such a family breeds a love security in which children can live—a retreat from all the insecurities of the community and the world.

Along with the love parents have for each other, of course, is that extension of love to the children. The average child will ask five hundred thousand questions before he gets into high school. And parents have the privilege of answering them! I say it is a privilege because no one wants his children to get the answers elsewhere. We want them to come home. If we take the time and they know parents will give them an answer within a love context, they will feel secure enough to keep coming back.

The next thing needed is a supportive system, a reinforcement system, to the children and to each other. Parents need to give children appreciation and praise. Sir Walter Scott as a boy was a very, very poor student. In those days in Scotland they used the dunce cap and the stool for punishment, and almost daily Scott would sit for some period of time in the corner wearing the dunce cap. He came to think of himself as a really dull, useless person, someone in the way, not destined to get anywhere in life. He dragged along behind his class. He did not like who he was.

Then one day, when Scott was twelve years old, he was at a home where some of the literary celebrities had gathered. They were talking together about some of the things going on in that part of the world. Robert Burns was there. Burns was looking at a painting. As he examined it, he read a little couplet at the bottom of the painting. He turned about and said, "Does anybody know where this couplet came from?" No one could answer his question.

After everyone had gone back to their conversation, Walter Scott went over to Burns and said, "Mr. Burns, I can tell you where the couplet came from." He recited the whole poem to Mr. Burns.

Afterward, Robert Burns laid a hand on the boy's head and said, "Aye, laddie, the time will come when you will be a great man in Scotland." From that moment the life of Walter Scott changed.

Someone had given him a vision of what he could become, and he realized all at once that he was meant to be a significant part of God's world. That beautiful monument on Princess Street in Edinburgh in his memory now bears witness that he achieved that goal.

Families need a security system as well as a support system. But finally a spiritual system is needed. Parents need some way to get to the heart of their children. Someone has called it organic communications. That is to say, parents should not only teach the facts but live them. The children will see the truth unfold before their eyes. Knowledge is not just transmitted for what it is—but because it is believed. It is not something the child has to learn by the time he grows up. It is something by which parents solve their problems in life. The child sees it in a minute and comes to recognize that when mom and dad and the family are in trouble, they come together and pray. When there are good times, they thank God. They know the Author of all things. They know to whom they are ultimately responsible.

How do parents cultivate that? Probably with some creative way of family devotions—some way of setting aside time every single week, preferably a few moments every day, when they read and pray together. How will the children learn to pray if they never hear parents pray or never hear them cry out to God and say, "I need your help," or, "Thank you, Lord, for all the blessings I enjoy"? If they never see their parent's enthusiasm for Christ, why should children be enthusiastic? If they never see parents giving the first fruits, the best they have, then after all, God must only be second place.

One of the finest things parents can do for their children is to bring them to church where the family can have a common experience. Once a week they worship together and return home and talk about the subject together. Children need to sing with dad and hear mother express her faith. Worship then becomes part of their way of life, and they see parents enjoying it. A spiritual system, with the support system, and the security system—all three are needed to reemphasize and build on the truth that your children are really a heritage of the Lord.

There is nothing finer for this country nor for our world than the family. There is nothing we need more to stabilize our society than this anchor, this place where we can all retire each day, to find security and support, and spiritual strength. How blessed are we if our parents knew, when we were young, that we were a heritage of the Lord! How marvelous it is today to know that our families can recognize that God is among us and that we can build with enthusiasm because of his presence. The family is God's great gift. Let us make this resource what it ought to be.

Successful Parenting

It is difficult to be a parent. Every serious parent struggles with it. Many articles are written on the subject, seminars held, and a great deal of wise advice given. But there is also some advice being given that is not so wise. We have to pick and choose what is best for us.

Children today are bright and thought-provoking. But the task of parenting is in principle what it always was. Scripture gives some very basic and unchanging guidelines. It tells us, in the first place, in Psalm 127, that children are a heritage of the Lord. That is, we as parents are representing God. It is his children we are rearing. It is in his interests that we train them. If we are going to be good parents today, it will be because of our loyalty to God and because we want our children to honor him by reminding them of the things he has done in history and is doing in the world today.

Our children are very special because they are made in the image of God. They were created unlike anything else in the world, unique in themselves but also unique in kind (Gen. 1; Eccles. 7). Our children have a right to our respect. They have a dignity in themselves.

In Psalm 139, the Psalmist extolled the tremendous potential of a little child, the wonders of God's hand and his work. Even before birth, a child is designed by God with all of the talents and abilities and potential that God wants and that he intends to use. It is up to the parents to fashion, to develop, to nurture, and to tend that child in order that those potentials become a reality.

Parents are not only responsible for the welfare and the care of the child but also for their spiritual and mental development. Parents are the prime educators. In Genesis 18 we read of a covenant established with Abraham. The reason God established the covenant was so that Abraham would teach his children about God's plans which would take place in history. It is through the people of God that the Holy Spirit moves and that things happen for good. God accomplishes what he wants to accomplish as generations continue to seek him, to submit to him, and to follow his ways.

In Deuteronomy 6, we have a direct mandate as to the way in which we are to train our children. Parents are to be educating when they retire and when they get up, when they are sitting in their homes and when they are busy in the marketplace or walking in the way. Their position is to be written on the doorpost for the community to see. It is also to be inscribed in their own hearts. The finest way to teach, as we all know, is by example, exposure, and companionship day after day. In that manner a little child absorbs a way of life. Truth must be more than taught. Truth is to be lived by parents. The parent is involved in those things that he verbally teaches his children are correct and right. There is to be a harmony between what is said and what is done. Most of the time we do not have time to say it, so we simply do it. Little children watch and hear.

There is no fad and no gimmick that will ever satisfy this description in Deuteronomy 6. We can attend all the seminars and make all the outlines we wish. But the fact remains that Christian parents need to spend their time living a life that is in keeping and in harmony with what the Scriptures teach. We need to take time to develop a life-style consistent with a biblical philosophy of life. We need to absorb God's mind so that his mind will be our mind and our mind his mind. A child will come to know simply because of exposure and involvement in the process. That is the ideal.

A recent magazine article was entitled, "What My Parents Did Right." After reading it, I took the time to write down an outline of what I thought my parents had done right. I found the exercise so valuable that I recommend others to do it too. I ask them to make a list of these things and then to check them against what they are doing. There will also occur to them many things that were left undone or done wrong. But it does give an idea of where we are in the whole process of parenting.

The value of nurturing is found in many places in Scripture. For example, God came to Solomon and asked what he would choose if he could have anything in the world. Solomon wrote in Proverbs 4 that he sought wisdom because of what his parents taught him.

Research tells us that 50 percent of a child's personality is formed between the years of one and four. Another 30 percent is formed between the years of four and eight. Eighty percent of a child's disposition toward life is fashioned by the time he is eight years old! Much of this time is in the home with parents where a child listens and watches or at home with someone whom the parents designate. We must be extremely careful what influences them because God holds parents responsible. What it also means, of course, is that the schools are the extension of the home, that for formal education the teachers represent the parents. But in the eyes of God it is the parents who are finally responsible, not the teachers in the schools, nor the church.

What can we expect from our children? Some people say, "Not much. They are sinners—born to sin, totally depraved." These people paint a very dark, black picture of what children really are. They add, "If you don't believe it, just let them go when they are one, two, or three years old and see what they get into."

There are others who say, "Oh, no. That is not true. Children are good. They are innocent. It is our bad behavior, our example, and the environment that does it to them. It is not in the genes."

So opinions polarize. On the one hand, some believe that parents need to discipline, that there must be a strong hand of authority. But the other opinion is that parents need to be permissive, to let the child's own personality emerge without parents detracting in any way.

Perhaps both opinions are right. There has to be authority on the one hand but some permissiveness on the other hand. This truth is found also in Scripture. In Ephesians 6 Paul wrote to the children: "Obey your parents in the Lord, for this is right" (Eph. 6:1). That is the side of discipline and authority. Then Paul turned to parents on the other hand: "Fathers, do not provoke your children to anger" (6:4, RSV). What that means is that we should not be too heavy-handed with our authority. We should give them some freedom.

As we ponder the examples of Scripture that teach us how to parent, we see that we really ought to exercise authority as we shape our children's lives. Then we must gradually release that authority so that a child may mature and finally come to complete freedom from the parents and stand on his own, making his own decisions. There must be, therefore, that period of training which includes both discipline and limited freedom.

The wisdom we pray for is to know when to exercise authority and when to set free. The Scripture has something to say about it. First of all, it tells us that we are to discipline our children when they are unreasonable or irrational. We must deal with the child's problems so that he does not hurt himself and so that he may develop an internal understanding and discipline whereby he helps himself through the rough places and avoids the pitfalls which we know are there. Scripture says, "He that spareth the rod hateth his son; but he that loveth him chasteneth him" (Prov. 13:24). The Scripture says, "Chasten thy son while there is hope, and let not thy soul spare for his crying" (Prov. 19:18). In other words, parents should not get emotional because children become emotional when hurt by discipline. Expect it, but do not worry about it, says Scripture. "The rod and reproof give wisdom: but a child left to himself bringeth his mother to shame" (Prov. 29:15). "Correct thy son, and he will give thee rest; yea, he shall give delight unto thy soul" (Prov. 29:17). "Train up a child in the way he should go, and when he is old, he will not depart from it" (Prov. 22:6).

Discipline is difficult for some of us. We are not quite certain that power and love go together or that the kind of force that we need to exert in discipline is a part of the caring we should express as Christians. The problems arise as the child begins to reach the years when the teachers, the den mothers, the scout master, the counselors, the coaches, television, the youth leaders, and his peers tell him what to do.

Parents must not be lacking in confidence. Remember, God holds them responsible. The child looks to parents to set and to maintain the standards. They find their security in parents who know what the standard is, who articulate it, who expect it, and who enforce it.

The Scripture says that if one wants to know what kind of training has gone on in the past generation, look around. One will see in the present youth what has happened in the past. Eli in the Old Testament was a good example, as were Isaac and David. Lack of discipline brought shame and loss of temporal things as well as disaster to their children.

Freedom, maturity, adulthood—these are the goals for which we push the eaglet out of the nest. Parental wisdom is an intuitive knowledge to set the child progressively free as the child has the ability to deal with life. It takes a great deal of wisdom which many people cannot handle. They never set their children free, even in college or post-college or marital years. Psychologists say that there are three kinds of parents that hang on. The persecutor type lays down the law and tells a child exactly what he has to do and gives him a guilt complex for disobedience if he does not do it no matter how old the child is. There is the victim type, the "poor me," who says, "Look at all I have done for you, and this is the way you treat me. You don't listen to me any more." Then there is the rescuer type who always comes to the aid of a child who is going to fail and never lets the child learn through failure and hardship.

The difficult years, I suggest, are those junior high and high school years when children begin to turn away from parents toward the peer group or toward independence. They ask questions and seek the liberty and the release that they want. Parents need the wisdom to know when children can handle limited freedom. When have their children's loyalties matured toward God? When have they been released from the loyalties to man, the peer group, and the pressures of the day? When these occur, parents can set them free with confidence.

How do we release them in college years, post-college years, marriageable years? Would we dare do what the father did with the prodigal? There was a great example of confidence in a young adult. Father knew his son was wrong. The father probably could see in his mind's eye exactly what would happen to his fortune if he turned it over to his son. But he gave it to him. He taught the son enough so that, when his son failed miserably with material things, spiritually he still knew enough to come back home. The father was willing to say, "Take what I have materially. And if you lose it, the benefit to your spiritual life, the lessons you will learn, the character that will result from this situation will be more than enough compensation." When the son came home, the father accepted him and threw a party. Would you do as much? It is difficult to let go and to believe that those young and inexperienced, tender children know enough to handle life. Yet the years of discipline, if they are to prove fruitful, must flow into the years of freedom when one finds the rewards of parenthood.

Life can be divided into three parts. The first part is one's own experience of going through the process of becoming mature, of becoming an adult. The second period of life is when we become responsible for helping God's children who are entrusted to us to go through that same process. The last third of life is when we enjoy the fruit of our efforts. Those whom we have helped are grateful, and their lives demonstrate that kind of discipline and the kind of freedom that we have bequeathed. We give to the next generation that which is ours, and then we rest in God's promise of blessing.

Today we thank God, the Father, for his wonderful guiding principles. And we thank God, the Son, for his wonderful Church which supports and helps us in parenting. We thank the Holy Spirit who lives within to give us that intuitive wisdom to know when to let go of discipline and to allow the young life to grow in a context of competent freedom.

Creative Fatherhood

We treat our lives much like a light aircraft. When the weather is clear and the air is calm, we fly along rather comfortably. If on occasion the compass needle tells us we are a bit off course, we move over a bit or the tower may warn us. It is when the gales are howling and the winds are blowing and it is cloudy and foggy that we stay close to our controls. We are thankful for those controls, and we are thankful for radio and radar. It is by these means that we find our way safely to our destination.

Families fly somewhat the same way. When it is clear and rather calm, the controls are on automatic. We are not overly conscious of them. If we get off course, we are nudged back by observation or perhaps by a friend. Or, it might be a neighbor, a relative, a preacher—somebody telling us that we are going in the wrong direction. But in these days of turbulence, when we ought to be watching the controls more closely than heretofore, very often we do precisely the opposite.

In the day of so-called nuclear families, we think it is our right to be independent and to fly along by ourselves. We hesitate to nudge a friend or neighbor to get him back on the pattern. We just hope everybody somehow makes it. Through all of the relativism and the tumultuous changes of our time, families find it difficult to reach their destination. What we need, I believe, is to get our fathers back in the cockpit. We need to consider once again the Scriptures to discover exactly what fathers are supposed to be. The Bible says that the glory of our children lies with father (Prov. 17:6).

Some schools of psychology and anthropology teach that the idea of the fatherhood of God is simply a projection of something that we think we need. So, we create this idea of fatherhood, extend it to a divine being, and then trust him. One observation we can make about their statement is that at least they recognize the innate need of fatherhood. If everyone needs a sense of fatherhood and, if the father is good, then he is the glory of his children. If fatherhood finds its definition in the proper place, then the father can accomplish this purpose. But if he has no rudder by which to steer, and if he has no star to guide him, then we are all lost, and the idea of fatherhood becomes meaningless.

Christians look at fatherhood in a different way. Fatherhood is not something that man has conjured up and then related to God. It is not an anthropomorphism anchored in us and then projected to God to help us understand him. We find, rather, that God in eternity is a Father, always has been a Father, and that the characteristics of God himself are those which he gave to his heirs. He bequeaths those qualities to those who bear his image. Our fatherhood is defined in his Fatherhood. Once we get the cart and the horse in the right perspective, we begin to see that, if we are going to be good fathers, then our definition is found in God.

Paul wrote to the Ephesian church that God is the Father of all mankind, the whole earthly family, and he always has been (Eph. 3). In him we find the definition, so we look to him to find understanding.

What does it mean to be a father? How does God define fatherhood? How has he practiced fatherhood through the years? If we look to his nature as our definition, we discover first of all that he is loving. In the Apostles' Creed we confess that we believe in God the Father Almighty. That God is sovereign and almighty might mean one thing. That he is a father says something entirely different. It says that, in his fatherliness, he will apply his sovereignty. He will love us though he is sovereign. He will not only rule us absolutely; he will rule us as a father. That means that he will love us, he will be concerned with us as individuals. He will not always rush to stop those things that we initiate even though they may hurt us. He respects our personality and our privacy. As we stumble along the way, he is not always going to guard. He will let us err and fail. He may be like the prodigal's father who said, "Very well, son, here is your inheritance," knowing all the time what was going to happen because he knew his child.

As Father Almighty, God could rule us and dictate every move to us, but in his love he wants us to be identifiable as individuals. He is like an earthly parent who coaches and counsels, but who watches. As children hurt themselves, the father is always there to pick them up and to help heal the wounds and set them back on track. He is the prodigal's father who warmly welcomes the son home. He brings forgiveness to the repentant. He says, "Come unto me." He rushes out on the road to greet and in his grace he pursues and does not always wait to be pursued. The God of love, the forgiving Father, would have earthly fathers to be what they are meant to be.

Every earthly home ought to reflect that kind of love. Fathers ought to be lovers, who are as dynamic in their love as God was in his when he sent his Son. Their love ought to be in the home because they are also a part of the home. Love is not just for mothers. Nor is love something that is pure sentimentality. The love of God was anything but that. His love was strong, as we could expect from God. He loved so strongly that he gave his Son.

An article by Charlie Shedd about fatherhood began in his typical fashion: "Answer me quick, what is your number one job as a father?" If we had to choose the number one job of fatherhood, what would we say it is? Shedd answered, "The number one job of my fatherhood is to love my children's mother." That is where the strength of fatherhood lies.

My parents were rather private people. We children did not see a great deal of the romantic side of their marriage. But on occasions I would come into the kitchen unexpectedly and find them in an embrace. I remember I would quietly let the old swinging door between the dining room and kitchen close and hope they did not see me because I was embarrassed even more than they would have been. But as I slipped out, I felt good because I knew that father and mother were lovers, that there was a stability in the home that was supporting all that was said. What greater need does a young person have today than for that sense of security? In that embrace of love I saw in the kitchen was a family where love was exposed and where even as a small boy I

knew for certain that my parents were the basic participants.
God our Father first of all loves. Our homes ought to be strong
because the father loves the children's mother and then
expresses his love to their offspring. They should know that behind
the sternness and the busyness of fathers there lies a heart which
is like God's own. That kind of father is a glory to his children.

But that love is much more than sentiment and emotion. It is
also a love of discipline. The heavenly Father's love sees life as it
truly is and makes certain demands which will be helpful to the
child. The Scriptures say that if there is not chastisement, children
are not considered sons, (Heb. 12:8) for God chastises those
whom he loves (Heb. 12:6). It also tells us that if we spare the rod
we hate our children (Prov. 13:24). God never spared the rod. It
is not recorded in the Scriptures that God agreed to discipline and
then compromised his position.

Today we seem to think that love means "anything goes," an
attitude that says, "If you love me, you will not discipline me."
But according to the Scriptures, God disciplines *because* he loves.
Is there a more insecure person than the child who does not
know when he is doing right because he never knows when he is
doing wrong? He is never quite certain when something is well
done because he never knows when it is not well done.

God has taught, since the Garden of Eden, that there are some
rules for life. In his own sense of justice and discipline the
Scriptures tell what happens when we disobey and what happens
when we obey. When there was disobedience, there was no
compromise on God's part and no other chances given. Adam
and Eve knew in advance what was going to happen. And the Bible
shows us that every word we say will be accounted for one day.
God will hold us responsible for every deed. And there is no room
for compromise. Inexorably the house built on sand will
disappear in the time of the flood waters. There is no way we can
begin to pray in midstream when we have not placed the
foundations deeply enough. God loves and forgives but he seldom
reverses the consequences of our disobedience.

Eli, the Old Testament priest, discovered this truth with his own
sons. They literally became the death of him. He refused to
discipline, apparently thinking his leniency was his expression of
love. But in his old age he died because of the betrayal of his
sons. What a sad story when an aged man recognized that he

couldn't go back and pick up the pieces, that his definition was wrong from the beginning!

Fathers must emulate God in matters of discipline. They must find ways to discipline that also speak of justice. In my home, it was always considered a privilege when we were allowed to use the family car. But there was also responsibility involved. I knew that if I broke or violated the rules, there were going to be some unpleasant results. But they prepared me for other times of judgment and assessment of self-conduct. Later when my college president called me in and said, "Arthur, you have broken some of the rules on the campus. Because you are chairman of the student council, I will have to make a public example of you. Now what do you think your punishment ought to be?"

That kind of question brought me up short. What do you think God ought to do when we violate his commandments? A child knows what a parent ought to do. When it is done in love and when it is done so that there is a balance between the discipline and the disobedience, there is no cause for remorse and bitterness.

One of the greatest texts in the Book of Proverbs is: "He who is slow to anger is better than the mighty, and he who rules his spirit than he who takes a city" (16:32, RSV). A child's glory is a father who teaches him how to rule his spirit. He teaches how to turn off lust, how to settle for a hard day at work, and then maybe some more work on top of that. He will teach his child that there are disciplines in life. This kind of father walks in the steps of God. It is difficult to rule one's spirit. But if one does not learn it in childhood, when will he ever begin to practice it? It is very difficult to learn as a young adult how to control one's spirit. Fathers must be disciplinarians who can teach their children self-discipline.

The love and discipline roles of fatherhood are seen in the nature of God as he teaches them to us. God has a program for the way this teaching works out in our lives. In Ephesians 1 we read a little bit about the program, how that from all eternity God had plans for us, not only for the human race but for us as individuals. God the Father so loved us that he came to us in his own Son. "We beheld his glory—glory as of the only begotten of the Father, full of grace and truth" (John 1:14). God was incarnate in Christ partly that we may learn of him. And his program was to send his Son to redeem us for himself and to get us once again on the right track, to focus us on what it means to live as he would have us live.

Fatherhood is part of his plan, and fathers are working under the authorization of God himself. This is his idea — not ours. Some people today talk as if we created the idea of the family and that we are the ones responsible for the roles of mothers and fathers and children. God is the One who revealed himself as a father. Christ used the term over a hundred times, almost once for every page in the New Testament, so essential was it that we understand this concept of fatherhood. God manages by objectives. He does not simply let us float through history, hoping we will come some day to the right port. No! Rather, he has laid his plan and fatherhood is a part of it.

God gave a certain authority to fathers. In the conversation of Jesus with the centurion, they talked about authority. Christ received his authority from his Father. The centurion received his from Rome. Both could give a command and it would be obeyed. But they could only give their orders on the basis of the authority delegated to them from another source. So it is with fathers. Their authority is not their own; it is rooted in God through Christ. They cannot assume it as their own. They must listen to have the mind of God running through their love, their justice, their discipline. They must not provoke their children to wrath. God does not and they must not. But in this limited sense they are to practice fatherhood.

Children will find their loyalty in father's authority under God. If fathers are not the authority, children will find it elsewhere in their community. And in today's community it can come from anyone. With community morals and values changing each decade, children without the authority of a father have no stability. They desperately need the authority which their fathers should give them.

Fathers need to take an interest and give attention to how they teach values, and how they communicate love, fairness, self-discipline, responsibility, and patience. Men do not deal with their vocations in a haphazard manner. They carefully plan. They do not rush headlong into a move, but they think, pray, and discuss. Fathers deal with other human lives entrusted to their care, but many today have a terrible time finding hours for the family. But do not tell me it cannot be done, because I know many busy fathers who are doing it. Some who are the busiest are doing it well. It is a matter of deciding that it has to be done. It can be done because we can do whatever we think is a top priority on our schedules. Let us be honest; fatherhood must be given a much higher priority than many have assigned it.

The tone fathers set is going to be the tone of the next generation. It was so in biblical times. In 2 Samuel 18 we find one of the saddest tales in the Bible. The father's name was David, and he reared a son named Absalom. David wept for his son. But the boy did exactly as his father had done. Absalom lusted and took a woman who was not his to claim. His father, David, had done the same thing. David wept with a broken heart at the death of that undisciplined son. Although David had many virtues, he was not the world's greatest father, and he suffered for the poor example he had set.

Most have many memories of our fathers. My father had a hardware store and went to work every morning before I got out of bed and he came home for a late supper. He never complained, always worked hard, and was thankful for what he had. He had many friends that were more well-to-do than he was. But I never heard a jealous word from him, for he always said, "Just be thankful with what you have, for God has blessed us."

Of the many things he taught me, I remember one incident which gave me something to ponder later in life. He used to take time off to work in his yard. When I got old enough, I worked with him. I saw how he seeded the lawn in the spring and fertilized it, cleaned the flower beds and edged them, and then sprinkled the lawn. We lived in Michigan where the soil was quite sandy, and it needed a lot of water. We mowed the lawn every week and swept the sidewalk and trimmed the edges.

When I was about nine years old, Mr. Hendrikson from down the block came and said, "Arthur, will you take care of my lawn this summer? You do such a nice job on your own."

I was proud. Dad was not doing it anymore; I was doing it alone. And now I was going into business. So I said to my dad, "I'm going into business."

He said, "That's fine. What are you going to do?"

I answered, "I'm going to take care of Mr. Hendrikson's lawn. He is going to give me a dollar a week for twelve weeks. He is going to the lake all summer."

"Well," he said, "then let's wait until the end of the summer before you take the $12."

I said, "Oh, I was planning to spend it."

But Dad said, "We had better see what the lawn looks like at the end of the summer. The reason you got that job was because of this job. I want to see you be just as proud of his lawn as you are of ours. Forget about the money. You never work for money, Art. You work for the satisfaction of doing something well for someone who is looking to you to do it well."

"Good," I said. "Then I will get the $12 at the end of the summer."

And he replied, "Yes, and it goes in the bank."

And it did. I worked all summer and learned about doing a job well, about pleasing someone else, and about being thankful that I could please someone else. I learned to forget about the remuneration, which always takes care of itself. And it always has. Lessons learned like that are not forgotten when we grow older. We are not always conscious of them, but as I was writing this, I was thinking about those days. How many little things have added up to the big things of life! How many things one absorbs from associations! I think my father knew what he was teaching me. We have to think about giving our children the best thoughts we have and letting them see in us good examples of how to deal with life and how to be a good trustee before God.

One thing a father can do for his children is to bring them to worship on Sunday morning. Children have to know that father is serious about worship. So he sings off key! He means what he sings and that is what counts. Young people need to see what is important to their parents. They want to know that father is giving to the church and why. How important do our children think God's work is in their community and elsewhere in the world? What kind of system do we have or do we have one? Children sometimes prompt us to think seriously about why we are doing what we are doing.

Father is the glory of his children if he spends time and reflects the character of God in the life he leads. God should be in the center of his life, important to him, documented not only by his words but by his deeds.

General Douglas MacArthur had many thoughts about parenthood. He once said, "By profession I am a soldier and take pride in that fact. But I am more proud, infinitely more proud, to

be a father. A soldier destroys things in order to build. The father
only builds, never destroys. The one has the potentialities of death;
the other embodies creation and life. While the hordes of death
are mighty, the battles of life are mightier still. My hope is that my
son, when I am gone, will remember me, not for the battles, but
in the home repeating with him our simple daily prayer, 'Our Father
who art in heaven.' "

A Mother's Legacy

A speech was recently given by William E. Ross, the president of J. Walter Thompson, Inc., in which he quoted a Yankelovich study. It said that three out of four parents today have added a plank to the Bill of Rights of this nation: Parents are entitled to self-fulfillment and self-actualization and self-realization. Because of this, parents are requiring alternative caretakers of their children. One of them is television, and another is the growing service of publicly financed day-care centers.

For many years we have been telling each other that self-fulfillment is the way to go. A recent article in *Look* magazine by Rollin, one of the editors, was titled "The Motherhood Myth." Rollin said that the real truth we have to learn is: "Be fruitful; don't multiply." Somehow we have the idea that motherhood today is less desirable than we knew it to be when we were kids. In fact, according to Rollin, there is likely to be a growing demand for the government to intervene in a quasi-parental role to preserve the family. It is interesting that the government should have to recognize the value of motherhood at a time when so many individuals are saying it is no longer a requisite to happiness and the fulfillment of our national destiny.

Today's world is challenging many of the concepts of motherhood that have been held fairly constant for many centuries. I remember when I was a boy, my mother used to spoil a lot of my fun. I had to do things like wash my hands, wash behind my ears, and take baths. I had to scrub my teeth twice a day and go to the dentist. I had to go to bed at 7:30 P.M. in the wintertime, just when the Lone Ranger came on the radio. Then in the summertime when it became dark outside and all the fun started, I had to be home. The other kids were out in the neighborhood doing the things that I wished I was doing.

Mother also made me scrub her floors, both bathroom and kitchen. I had to learn to dust her furniture. I even ironed handkerchiefs and pillow cases. I had to go to school without fail, walking over a mile in any kind of weather. I had to come right home after school. Mother would always be there to check up on me. I had to change my clothes before I went out to play. She had a stick in the kitchen drawer about three quarters of an inch square. I knew where it was. I also knew why it would be used. I often made my choices on the basis of what I wanted to do and what the stick would say. But mother was always just and fair, but firm. She let me go to movies, but I had to come home and discuss with her what I saw. Then we would decide whether the movie was good or bad and whether it built character or destroyed it.

She always took me to church. Even if I did not know what was going on, I had to be there with the family and be very quiet and still. Many times that is what provoked the use of the stick. We also had what we called in those days catechism lessons. From the third grade on, once a week, I went to learn the answers to questions about the Bible. Mother was always there at the door waiting to listen to all those answers before she would let me go to class. She taught me to save and to spend carefully, to give 10 percent of it back to the Lord and to be happy I could do so.

I saw her role in the home not only as my mother but as the lover of my father. She did not always agree with him but she always supported him. The two of them had something going between them that I did not understand when I was young. I knew they were happy and that they admired each other. In the context of that love I grew up and built my own expectations of the home I would have one day.

I remember my mother as she worked hard in times of depression when we were poor. She fried eggs and potatoes for the tramps that came in off the street. She went to help the sick and practiced what we would call "plain neighborliness and love."

She read Bible stories to me and taught me to pray. I learned to know that she meant every word that she said to God. It was the beginning of a confidence that I, too, could build on the One who had given me life.

She died twenty-four years ago when I was just a young preacher. She left four children, who were all married, and all of us have stayed married. We all have some of the ideals that we learned from her. Coming from good homes, her grandchildren get along together. Her family is happy together. Yet, somehow the kind of mother I had is suspect today. Why should it be?

Look at some of the concepts of motherhood that come from the Scriptures. Christians live in the context of tensions arising between the contemporary ideas of motherhood and the teachings of the Scriptures. In the Old Testament there is recorded a beautiful prayer of a woman named Hannah, who was married to Elkanah. He was a middle-class entrepreneur, having vast flocks and herds. But in spite of all his wealth, he also wanted the wealth of children, for sons and daughters represented to him the continuation of his own influence. In his society children gave him a place among his peers. But Hannah could give him no children. Her barrenness was a frustration to her, for she wanted to be a good wife. So she prayed to God, "Lord, I want to be a good wife. Let me bring children to Elkanah."

For twenty years God said nothing. So, Elkanah married Peninnah, a second wife who gave him children. As a result, dissension developed in his home much like that in the home of Abraham. One wife was barren, and the other one was able to bear children for the husband. In that context there was a contest for position. Elkanah, who wanted Hannah to know how much he loved her, pledged to her a double portion of anything he gave to Peninnah. Somehow material compensation as evidence of caring and love was not enough. Hannah kept praying to God.

They lived in a time when culture was deteriorating, according to the Book of Judges. The crime rate was on the rise and immorality was rampant. It was due, says the Scripture, to special interest groups which were pressuring the government to make laws to suit them, not caring for the nation as a whole. It was also a time when foreign people in the land, particularly the Philistines from the west, were bringing some of their low moral standards and religious practices into Israel. The people were participating in pagan ceremonies which penetrated even to worship in the tabernacle. Eli, the priest who took care of the tabernacle services, had two sons who became exceedingly immoral and exploited the privileges of their priesthood. Throughout the land there were few people like Elkanah and Hannah, who went regularly to the tabernacle to pray. They were diligent to pay homage, give their tithes, worship through their sacrifices, and recognize God as their Lord. At that time leadership was sorely needed in the country. Hannah continued to pray.

After twenty years there was a distinct change in the things for which Hannah asked. She had always asked for a son to honor her husband. Finally, after twenty years she prayed, "Oh, God, if you will give me a son, I will give him to you for your purposes, not for mine or those of my husband."

Then God answered, "That is a fair request." He then gave her a child. Think of all the pain that Hannah endured as she trained the child, knowing that it would not be long before she would have to give him up. She had covenanted with God, "If you will be a God to me, I will be a mother for you." In training the boy she taught him all that she knew about her spiritual life. She taught him to honor God and his fellow man, how to pray, and to dedicate his will to God who gave him life.

When the boy was old enough, she brought him to the tabernacle and said to the old priest, "Eli, treat him like your son. Help him to become a servant of God, for I promised I would give him back to the Lord when he became old enough to take care of himself." So when he was still a very young boy, she left him with Eli the high priest and returned to her home. The boy's name was Samuel, and as you know, he became a great prophet.

In due time God called Samuel. Later the prophet anointed and ministered to the first king of Israel, Saul, as well as to the second king, David. Samuel's name became synonymous with godliness and integrity. It was Hannah's son who was to grow up and be the leader in Israel and bring the people back to God. Samuel shaped the thinking of the nation just as his own thinking had been shaped at the knee of his mother.

Every year his mother would make a new garment from the wool of her husband's sheep. As the little lad grew, Hannah came at feast time and put the new garment on her son. The garment that he wore served as a reminder that his mother still cared, still loved him, and was still praying for him. It must have often kept him from temptation to know that his mother's love and concern was there and that her God was listening and watching.

We do not live in a much different time than Samuel's. Repeatedly in history we have seen that when God wanted a job done he did not have the government pass laws. Rather, he had children born who would become the leaders of nations.

Looking through the Scriptures, we will find evidence that God often used mothers to do his work. It happened in the very first two chapters of the Bible. Martin Luther stated it as well as anyone when he wrote: "When Eve was brought to Adam, he became filled with the Holy Spirit and gave her the most glorious of appellations. He called her Eve, that is to say, the mother of all living creatures. In this consists the glory and the most precious ornament of women."

All through the Scriptures we discover the importance of motherhood. Longfellow said, "Even He that died for us on the cross in that last hour, in the unutterable agony of death, was mindful of His mother as if to teach us that this holy love should be our last worldly thought."

John Calvin spoke of the Church as a mother who cares and who loves. Augustine, that wayward, immoral son of Monica, who was pursued by her prayers, was finally brought to the faith. After Monica had died, Augustine said, "It is the Church now to whose bosom I flee. There I find the love and stability that my mother gave me." That is a great goal and task for the Church. The Church's love is represented by motherhood.

Some people would like to say that women were especially unimportant in the Old Testament. I disagree. Women and mothers were extremely important. In fact, in the first four chapters of his prophecy, Amos had much to say about women and mothers in his land. For becoming disinterested in their primary task of raising their families, he said some rather unkind things about them. He claimed that they were demanding luxury and leisure, pushing their husbands to be productive so that they could take advantage of the prosperity. He said judgment would fall upon the nation unless women got back to their prime responsibility, that of caring for their children, the next generation. Amos said women set the trends of society. Certainly women are not unimportant!

Lord Shaftesberry wrote, "Give me a generation of Christian mothers, and I will change the face of all of society."

John Quincy Adams also said almost what Abraham Lincoln said: "All that I am, my mother made me."

Napoleon declared, "Let France have good mothers, and she will have good sons."

Thomas Edison commented, "If it had not been for my mother's appreciation and her faith in me at a critical time in my experience, I should never likely have become an inventor. I was always a careless boy. But her firmness, her sweetness, her goodness were potent powers to keep me on the right path. My mother was the making of me. The memory of her will always be a blessing to me."

It is recognized by most of us that our mothers had a great hand in getting us started on the right path. Their continuing prayers, the awareness of their desires, is such a strengthening factor in so many of our lives. Moses' mother is recorded as one who "nourished" him (Acts 7:20). The Greek word is *anatrepho,* which means "she formed his mind." She formed his ability to evaluate and analyze the things about him, developing his long-range view of life and its purpose. A mother brought up that little child who later led God's people from slavery to freedom.

Today we need mothers who will pray and fulfill their covenant relationship. We need mothers who pray, "God, give me a child, and I will raise that child for you." With that kind of attitude all our complaining would stop, since the child is not here to serve us. The child is not here to fulfill some thwarted ambition of our own. Our sons and daughters are here to do what God has in mind. It is a mother's destiny to stand in God's place. It was Mary, that young girl of Nazareth, who said yes to God where Eve had said no. Mary became the mother of God himself when he was incarnate on earth. God came through motherhood, blessed it, used it, sanctified it, and made it one of the most honorable and choice positions in the world.

Harold Blake Walker offered a challenge to mothers. He told of a young bride who wrote home after she was married and said, "You know what I mean when I say it is not what you did but the way you did it that matters. My gratitude will have to be shown by my being a good mother to my children." Real motherhood desires no credit but to honor God who has entrusted her with children. That is the joy and the challenge.

Our love and respect is offered to mothers. Our generation needs them. We Christians have high ideals for them, and we have a resourceful God. Mothers must look to God as Hannah did. He may seem to be silent for a time, but you can be sure he will answer. He will fulfill the purposes in our children that only he knows. Now more than ever before we need mothers to fulfill their sacred calling. We need Spirit-led mothers who will raise up children who will follow God and give us the kind of leadership we need in these trying times.

Teaching Meaningful Sex

No one would deny that our generation has a problem handling sex. The sociologists point out that 40 percent of the children born in Chicago are born out of wedlock. The only increase in the birth rate nationally in the last decade has been among girls ages eleven to fourteen. If the present trend continues, by 1985 half of the black mothers in Chicago will be unmarried and half of the black families of Chicago will be on welfare. These problems stem, they say, from the sex revolution.

Others tell us that the real problem is the lack of acceptance of these new standards or mores. The proponents of free abortions (of which there are over one million per year in the United States), the homosexuals, and the lesbians are quick to tell us that, although they have made some legal gains, they are not yet as accepted in our society as they desire to be. So they have formed their lobby and pressure groups. They angle to be seen on the media. They publish widely. They crusade. They want a voice. They demand attention.

Still others tell us that the need today is for an educational program. We must reach the young people, since they are the ones having trouble handling sex. What we think we need to do is help them make the right decisions.

Psychologists tell us that the sex problems of our youth relate to loneliness, to feelings of rejection, to the isolation engendered by this society. Young people want reaffirmation of

their self-worth and an experience of fulfillment. They are
finding it, they feel, in sexual experimentation. But they are
disappointed. Theologians tell us that sex is being used by them
with a purpose for which it was never intended. The conflict
between the pressure of the society and a Christian conscience
produces great tension. If the Christian indulges, he feels guilty.
And if a Christian restrains himself, he isolates himself from
society.

There are many more aspects to the misuse of sex and it does
us no good to hope that the problem will disappear. The problem
has existed in one form or another throughout the generations.
But when the abuse of sex is accelerated, it is always coincidental
with the demise of a culture. This causes us to pause, to do some
thinking, to ask some questions about what we ought to do.

The Creator has offered guidance. He has a purpose for sex,
something very different from some of the popular answers being
given. The question before us is, "How can we best serve our
fellow man and God?" The answer is, "By doing God's will through
our sex life." How can we support those around us and give
them not only good models but good guidance in the way they use
that trust?

First of all, I propose that we Christians look at the grid against
which we must measure, weigh, and evaluate what is going on in
society today. We have a most beautiful basic and undergirding
substructure which God has given. Sex to us is nothing alien. It is
something beautiful, and it has been given, in the first place, for
our pleasure. We read in the Song of Solomon that sex is
something that God gave to man (2:3, 6). Through sex, man
rejoices, finds expression for his love, and adds a totally unique
dimension of pleasure to his life. God takes the credit for sex.
Some people think that he often looks down, covers his eyes,
and says, "Oh, no! They are at it again." This is totally wrong, for
God intended it as a gift to be used properly, and he blesses his
people in the right use of it. Let us be neither embarrassed nor
mistaken, for God wants us to be fulfilled through the use of his
gift in marriage, our most intimate relationship.

This brings us to a second purpose: through marriage, God
binds us together in intimacy and responsibility. Those two
cannot be divided without destroying the purpose of sex, which
is reserved for a lifetime of commitment. When it is separated and

reduced to something less, then we are participating at a subhuman level. Sexual intimacy has the potential to weld together a relationship like nothing else on earth. It is a vital part of an intimacy that has nothing to do with individuality or personal privacy.

The animals need not identify themselves with names and commitments. There is no covenant for two animals that participate in the procreative act, as there is for human beings. We understand what we are doing. It must be part of that which binds us together in that one very private matter. From the beginning God made two human beings—male and female—and brought them together till death should part them. What God has joined together, as they become one flesh, man must not put asunder. That is why the Scriptures say that when a person joins himself to a prostitute, there is more involved than the physical act. They have literally joined souls, their persons. We talk a great deal today about wholistic health and wholistic psychology. We ought also to talk about wholistic sex. Sex cannot be isolated as a single act of a human being. It involves the whole person.

Thirdly, the purpose of sex is procreation. It is God's gift to two people who have given themselves in love to extend their feelings for one another through an intimate act which produces offspring. If all is healthy and well between two partners of a marriage covenant, then their children will be reared in an atmosphere that is most conducive to health and well-being. God knew exactly what he was planning. He gave to us what science is proving to us—that we cannot grow to be mentally, emotionally, or even intellectually healthy when there is tension, trouble, or animosity in the home. God meant lovers to have children. Blessed are those who are born into such loving, caring relationships.

These were some of the high ideals of God when he brought that first man and that first woman together. The fall came and man was alienated from the Creator. Man hid from the Lord. Work became drudgery. Nature became an adversary. Sex needed to be controlled. Man, we read, made a garment of fig leaves. God improved upon it when he took animal skins and covered man. Man needs to deal with sex in discipline and restraint. In the process of life he needs to control it in such a way that it becomes a blessing and not a curse.

As we read on through the Scriptures, we find six kinds of sexual practice which are condemned. The Bible has some very clear things to say about *bestiality,* about *homosexuality,* about *lesbianism,* about *incest,* about *prostitution,* and about *transvestism.* All are mentioned in the Scriptures as perversions of the purposes of God and this great blessing of sex.

Our society is struggling to understand how we can deal with the problems at hand in the light of our traditions. Western society basically has been built upon the Old and New Testament teachings about sex life. With this in mind, the State of Illinois in its Educational Advisory Committee set the following guidelines: "Premarital chastity is the standard for teenage sex behavior." That is a forthright statement with which we can all agree. It comes right out of the roots of our culture. We say, "Thank God for such a very clear-cut statement."

But that standard is not exactly what we see reflected in much that goes on today. For example, the educators in our schools in Illinois have decided we need to institute sex education to deal with the problem, so they planned to establish a curriculum for sex education. One organization stepped forward with such a curriculum — Planned Parenthood. They said to state educators, "We are ready; we understand the problem." So the Chicago Board of Education, like many boards across the country, spent thousands of dollars with Planned Parenthood and received other services from Planned Parenthood which were funded by the private sector, by HEW, and by other agencies of the federal government — millions and millions of dollars worth. Our Christ Church staff viewed one of their films because we are interested in what they are teaching our young people. After viewing the film, we began to question whether the Christian position, the historic cultural position, and our state guidelines are really being respected.

In a letter of June 12, 1980, signed by the coordinator of Family Life Education for the Board of Education in the City of Chicago, we read: "Because the goals and philosophies of Planned Parenthood are often contradictory to the guidelines of the Chicago Board of Education Family Life Educational Program and because of the political nature of their endeavors, [Planned Parenthood has been politically active in fostering free abortions, lesbianism, and homosexuality] the Chicago Public Schools have limited cooperation with Planned Parenthood." I do not know what "limited" means. Planned Parenthood people are not there all day, every day, with every student. But neither is any teacher. The fact is that the organization's philosophies have been accepted and funded.

I have read extensively from Planned Parenthood materials. A few illustrations will give some idea of the dimensions of the sexual revolution we face. In the curriculum for the senior high for 1980, a curriculum designed and paid for by HEW, we read about Cathy and Danny. They were dating, and, like all teenagers, there was a conflict between them. Danny wanted sex activities, but Cathy said no. So they struggled with this tension for a time and finally Cathy relented. The story illustrates that after Cathy relented and they became sexually active, there was great harmony between them which was good for their relationship. But then something happened. Cathy became pregnant. She had to tell her mother. Now the problem as portrayed in the manual was not that Cathy and Danny became sexually active; the problem was that Cathy became pregnant. The answer, therefore, is: "We must get birth control materials to our children in junior high and high school. We must educate them so that they can become sexually active and at the same time be nonproductive." That is Planned Parenthood's answer to the problem at hand and how they propose to train our children.

"Sexually active" is the term Planned Parenthood likes to use. In one of their recommended texts called *Our Body, Ourselves* we read that the loss of virginity, the loss of the state of purity and innocence, is viewed as a move from childhood to adulthood. "That is the way to grow up, young people. If you want to mature you participate," the book seems to say. In fact, another of their pamphlets called *Choices* states: "If you don't give sex, you run the risk of loneliness or frustration."

One pamphlet speaks to the girls and another to the young men. One such pamphlet reads: "Maybe you are caught up in the old mythology. The old mythology tells you that it is all right to give sex if you are married. If you have decided to be an old-fashioned girl, be it. Be it, but don't hassle other women who want something else." To the boys, "Do you want to marry a virgin? Buy one. There are girls in that business, too. Marriage is the price you pay, and you will get the virgin."

Could these teachings be called a neutral position in keeping with our western cultural position and the guidelines of our state? I fail to understand exactly how young people are not going to be confused in their minds as to the integrity and dignity that we have talked about in the three purposes of sex which Scripture defines. The promiscuity and the indulgences which are proposed and condoned by those who scorn the "old mythology" and the virginity of those who marry completely undermine our Christian standards.

It is not realistic to think that our young people, in their loneliness and their frustrations, are not looking for deep relationships. A medical doctor, Professor Collins at Syracuse University in New York, surveyed a group of college girls. Eighty percent of those who were involved in sexual activity intended to marry their partner. They were taking sex very seriously. To them sex was a commitment. It was more than experimentation or a way to reach maturity. It was part of the wholeness of the human being. We cannot, we must not, toy with what God has given for the most profound intimacies given us to enjoy. We have walked this road of insipid sexuality long enough. I think some of us ought to become concerned enough to do something about it. It is extremely frustrating to send our children to school and have them taught these things when we, in our homes and in our society at large, are committed to some far more profound and healthy practices.

Parents should become active in sex education. They should tell their sons how tender is the love of a young girl and not to abuse it. They should tell their daughter what she is surrendering when she engages in sex to find friendship or acceptance. Parents should invade the community process with their questions. They should probe, search, look at the curricula to which educators subject their school children. I invite parents who are capable, perhaps some young people who are looking for a career challenge, to become involved in designing a curriculum that will teach in accordance with what our state has said, our society says, and the Word of God says. All of us should take advantage of the programs in the church. Many churches have sex education programs that involve parents and Christian counselors.

The sexual revolution in our society means we can no longer afford to sit on the sidelines and bewail what is happening to us. We need to have compassion on a whole segment of our society that is helpless to help itself. We need to have compassion on our neighbors and our friends, as well as our own children, who are caught in the dilemma of conflicting ideals.

God help us to have a new appreciation of how the Creator from the beginning made us with great purpose and design to be in good health and productively to be male and female.

Relationships We Lose

God's creation was perfect. Marriage and parenthood as God designed them for man and woman were perfect. But sin entered the world and made the ideal creation to become far less than God intended it to be.

Imperfect bodies result in sickness, suffering, and death. Imperfect minds and emotions bring hurt and separations. Imperfect relationships bring loneliness, separations, and divorce.

Even through these imperfections God sovereignly has much to teach us — of grace to bear the losses and of his sufficiency to fill the void.

Is Divorce Ever Right?

Christian Century of May 5, 1971, published an article by Mary McDermott Shideler entitled "An Amicable Divorce." Two of her friends, whom she chose to call Matthew and Ann, had gotten a divorce. Mary had attended a small ceremony in their behalf and records for us the litany which read as follows: The audience says, "Oh, Lord, our Lord, how excellent is thy name in all the earth." And then, the one officiating read, "Dearly beloved, we have gathered here to solemnize the end of one time in Matthew and Ann's lives and the beginning of another. . . . Thirteen years ago the time was right for Matthew and Ann to be joined in holy matrimony. Then they needed for their growth in grace and truth the visible bond of marriage. Now the time has come when that bond is hampering both their growth as individual persons and their common life. They have resolved, therefore, to sever the ties of their marriage, though not of their mutual love and honor, and have asked us, their friends, to witness the affirmation of their new lives and to uphold them in their new undertakings." Thereupon, they relinquish the tie from each other. This ceremony was followed by a liturgical prayer of blessing and then a reception.

In 1976 this particular liturgy found its way into a new prayer book called *Renewal for a New Day — An Invitation*. The prayer book includes such things as forms for foot washing, for dying, and for moving to new locations. By including the divorce

ceremony in the prayer book, the church that uses it gives the
impression of sanctioning divorce. In this climate the
Bible-believing Church is asked to speak.

How one feels about divorce depends on how he feels about
marriage. If marriage is a social and a civil contract, then the
government and the society of which one is a part also can agree as
to when that contract is terminated. Today many people are
concerned with the community and its ability to forgive, to forget,
to accept. And in the Rogerian sense many ask, "Will we be
accepted if we divorce?"

A second question that follows is: "Can we afford to be
divorced?" When they think they will be accepted, and when they
can afford it, many people think it is time for a divorce.

On the other hand, others believe that marriage is something
different, that it has a permanency about it, that God is involved
in it, that one really has no right to believe that this covenant is for
less than a lifetime. Many have so pledged themselves in
marriage with complete sincerity. They recognize the permanence
of marriage. They seek to practice within its framework of love,
and are willing to accept the risk.

Now no matter what we may think about the subject, as
Christians, we ought to look to our Leader. It is important what
Jesus thinks. He did speak to the issue, and I would like to see
with you what he said. The subject is reported in Mark 10 and in
the parallel passage of Matthew 19.

The question the Pharisees put to our Lord was a trick question
to test him. "When is divorce right?" they asked. They asked
when it was lawful to get a bill of divorcement.

What the Pharisees were really trying to do was to get Jesus
involved in their own dispute, for there were two factions among
them. One followed Hillel, who was a very liberal Jewish rabbi.
He made many concessions beyond the Law of Moses and granted
divorce for many reasons. Shammai, on the other hand, was a
leading Jewish rabbi who was far more strict and adhered much
more closely to the letter of the Law of Moses. These Pharisees
were wondering whether Jesus would fall to the side of Hillel or
Shammai.

Jesus, however, did not answer their question. He confronted
these Pharisees who prided themselves on knowing the law by
asking, "What did Moses say?"

They quoted to him Deuteronomy 24:1, where Moses granted a bill of divorcement under certain conditions. Jesus then pointed out to them that the reason for that bill of divorcement was that in civil affairs there may be some concessions to the hardness of heart.

Jesus, however, refused to get involved in grounds for divorce. And he gave none! What he did, rather, was to refer them back to the time before God gave his laws or Moses penned the laws of the civil courts. He said that such a concession was not made at the beginning. Moses dealt with a sinful community and with the problems that arose in his time. But, at the beginning of time it was not so.

When God created man and woman, he created them in his image. Then he gave them the institution we call marriage in which the man and the woman become "one flesh." Old Testament research tells us that "flesh" means far more than a physical bond but also a total involvement of body and soul. That is God's purpose.

There is nothing in Genesis 2, which Jesus quoted, that gives the impression that there is any ground or basis for divorce. The Lord always preached the ideal. He never preached to accommodate sin. He always holds before us what we ought to be, not what we are. And so, at the end of the Sermon on the Mount, he says, "Be perfect, therefore, as your heavenly Father" (Matt. 5:48). He does not say, "Settle for your imperfections," or, "Make an excuse because of them."

The Lord gave God's definition and authority over marriage. Sin, for the present age, may dominate. But hardness of heart on the one hand is counter to God's ideal.

Christ's words cause some to say, "Then, Lord, it is not expedient for anyone to marry. It is too difficult for us to maintain a lifetime relationship at that high level (See Matt. 19:9, 10). God's standard, established at creation before sin entered the world, is not now possible. Christ reassured his disciples and us that, although none of us will ever achieve that high goal, yet by his grace and Spirit, we should work at it. We must submit ourselves to him, take him into our lives, and make him part of the marriage relationship.

Jesus said that marriage was permanent and any breaking of marriage was the result of sin in the world. That is the first thing he said about it. But the second thing he said was that man could find within this sinful world answers to his needs and hope for the future.

Jesus also met those who were adulterers. One of the incidents is recorded in John 4. He sat by a well just outside Sychar. There he met a woman who was married five times. She was then living adulterously with another man. He talked to her about who he was; and, when she made confession of her sin and need and reached out to him, he freely forgave her. And she became for him an evangelist to her people.

There is another incident in John 8, where Christ is confronted by the Pharisees with a woman who was taken in the very act of adultery. They wanted to stone the woman, in accordance with the law. But he said, "If you are without sin, cast the first stone." And one by one they departed until Jesus was left alone with the woman. And, he said to her (this perfect Man who might have thrown the first stone), "Neither do I condemn you. Go, and sin no more."

In the heart and mind of Jesus there was then also the command for repentance, an avenue of restoration and forgiveness. He took unto himself and into his Kingdom those who, as a result of sin, had broken the marriage bonds but who, as repentant image-bearers of God, were included among those for whom he would die, those whom he would redeem, those who could be forgiven and who could begin again a new life.

Applied to divorce, repentance means admission of sin and the aberration of the high ideal of God. It means a willingness, indeed a resolution, not to enter another relationship lightly without sincerely seeking the kind of love relationship and compatibility that will build a solid marriage. This kind of repentance means that one is set free but only to be in quest of that high ideal which is in the mind of God and with which he instituted marriage in the first place.

The two things, then, that Jesus said was that there is no ground for divorce. God meant marriage as a permanent relationship from the beginning. It is a sacred bond 'till death do us part. On the other hand, in a world of sin we deal with redemption and forgiveness and reconciliation. We can find a new wholeness in life through the forgiveness which comes through him.

If that is his teaching, what do we Christians say in the context

of what is happening in our society? We are living in an age
where the moral standards and the teachings of Jesus are not always
respected. Recently in the *Chicago Tribune* an education series
began on the subject of morality. The introductory lesson was
written by a Professor Philip Rieff, a sociologist at the University
of Pennsylvania. Some of his observations are very astute. He writes,

*In every culture guides are chosen to help men conduct
themselves through those passages from one crisis of choice
to another that constitute the experience of living. . . . Our
culture is in crisis today precisely because no creed, no
symbol, no militant truth is instilled deeply enough now to
help men constrain their capacity for expressing everything.
Internalizing values from an earlier period in our moral
history no longer holds good. Western men are sick precisely
of those interior ideals which have shaped their characters.
Accordingly, they feel they have no choice except to try to
become free characters and to believe that man is the supreme
being for man. What characterizes modernity, I think, is just
this idea that men need not submit to any power, higher or
lower, other than their own. It is in this sense that modern
men really believe they are becoming Gods.*

I think he is right. Our society, by mutual consent, determines
the standards of morality. Society permits some things and
condemns other things. When we are ready for change, it will
come, but not before. We are being conditioned constantly and
in a transitional age our standards are always changing. No
absolute authority is accepted. There is nothing above the
community standard that is established by the composite of
community opinion.

This means that man does what the community will accept. It
also means that man in so doing can become morally bankrupt.
Society permits men to respond to life without restraint. It now
condones abortion. One day it may approve prostitution. It may
approve gambling, and it may approve divorce. The opinion of the
community is molded by the support one gets from neighbors
and friends, the influence of what is read, of what is seen on the
screen or in a play. We, too, participate in the formation of
community-approved morals. But, if loneliness and brokenness

descend upon us, the community holds nothing to reestablish us. The community cannot redeem what we have lost. It can only say, "Well, go try again." And we probably will have the same results. Life becomes a tedious repetition.

This is where the Church breaks through with her very unique identity. The balance of the two things that the Lord taught become meaningful in his Church. In a society filled with brokenness, we must share the ideals and reconciliation of Christ.

The Church offers two dimensions. We profess to be a community with the mind of Jesus. In that community we see not only the high ideals of God, but also the forgiving grace that he offers. The two dimensions that are ours are the ideal and the discipline. The Church should never be afraid to say what is right, to take the position that Jesus took. This lends us guidance, gives us the mark toward which we shoot, sets up that light across the wave toward which our rocking boat will go.

But at the same time the Church teaches and administers the discipline of Jesus. It also says to those who are overturned in their small, frail bark on the waves of life, "Here is a life jacket. Come back into the ship. Find yourself once again surrounded by the love of those who have the mind of Jesus." The Church is the place of compassion and a place of forgiveness.

We are most realistic when we believe that Jesus can reclaim anything, including broken marriage. While divorce is never an ideal and marriage is always an ideal, we can rebuild with those who are divorced. There is a place for them, perhaps the only place for them left in this world, within the Church of Jesus Christ.

In our congregation we have an organization called the Re-Questors, made up of people who are divorced. It is a new quest, by the grace of God. The tension we feel as we study with and lead this group is that we cannot live with less than the ideal. We must never approve sin. Yet there must be forgiveness. Jesus came to live among us and to show us how to deal with such tension.

As married people we must be reminded of our responsibilities in marriage. It is a high ideal. We are practicing our relationship in a world of sin. We will never reach the perfect ideal. But we must work at it. With the help of Christ, our marriages can be beautiful.

Divorced people must be reminded of the love of Jesus Christ, of the redemption that he offers, and the new life and hope that he brings. But, also, they should be reminded of the need for repentance. A hasty duplication of sin is always forbidden. One ought to be extremely circumspect in looking for new relationships so that those relationships will be built on better soil than that which preceded.

Those who contemplate marriage or remarriage should be reminded that proper relationships are always under God and must be established with great care. There is much in the foundation and the beginnings that determine the achievement of ideals. Struggling to become citizens of the kingdom of God, we are deeply aware of our personal sins and those which are so commonplace in our world. We can rejoice together that, although no one is holy enough to cast the first stone, all of us in need can find forgiveness and redemption in Jesus Christ.

Why Do the Innocent Suffer?

Christians frequently ask the question, "Why do innocent people suffer?" Someone who isn't a Christian would probably never ask such a question since he would see all of nature as an adversary. He wouldn't ask God because to him God doesn't exist. But someone who believes in a good and sovereign God needs to know the answer.

As we live here on earth, we discover that our world can often appear to be more a chamber of horrors than a perfect creation. For one reason or another, certain areas suffer great discomfort. Huge areas are under the blight of pain and affliction, hunger, and disease. Much in our world speaks of anything but the love and goodness that we would expect from a world created by a good and loving God.

Senseless accidents, diseases, earthquakes, wars, and floods make us ask "Why?" If there is a sovereign God behind all of this, why the imperfection? We expect goodness, and we consider anything else as abnormal, a departure from the standard.

We look behind the suffering to see the cause, for we know that nothing in this world happens without a first cause. And as we go behind the cause of some immediate event, we come back to the ultimate being, God. We have come to know that the source of all things is a personal Being who is incarnate in Jesus Christ. Therefore, of him we ask, "Why?"

This leads us to the question of whether God is really responsible for the sin and suffering, the grief and the evil in the world. In one way he is not. He does not perpetuate it. He does not plan it. He does not design it. He is not there to administer it. And he takes no delight in it. Suffering is not on his agenda. He does not create it. So, in a sense, he is not responsible for it.

On the other hand, however, we may ask about his responsibility. Is he finally answerable? Can we find some understanding, some clue as to why it happens by asking him? And that is a different kind of question. All that happens in this world is beneath his sovereignty. At some point or other, there must have been a time when he was involved in something that has resulted in what we experience today — in this case, the suffering of the innocent.

We seek to find intellectual answers that don't always solve our emotional reaction to suffering, which we always find repulsive. No one likes war and disease, and we usually feel deep sympathy and compassion for those who suffer.

First we ask, "Has God accepted the misery of mankind? Is he passive toward it? Does he look upon it as something good?" To find the answer, we must ask another question about God's original intent when he created us. His world was beautiful — it was called a garden. There was balance in nature and harmony between nature and man. The two lived together in peace, prosperity, and health.

Man was meant to be the representative on earth of God in heaven. Man carried with him a likeness of both the material and the spiritual, an identity with both realms of reality. Man was meant to be trouble free. But then we read in Genesis 3 that he, of his own doing, decided to take upon himself the responsibility for his actions. In disobedience to his Creator, he decided to chart his own destiny. The result of his decision involved all of nature. Exactly how God brought it about we do not know. But we discover that Adam and Eve's wickedness, the greed, and the ambition and selfishness wreaked havoc upon all that God had created (Gen. 3:14-19).

Throughout the ages man has influenced nature so that the two are no longer in harmony with each other. No longer is man in harmony with himself or with his fellow man or with God. That disharmony resulted in suffering, in a bruised humanity. When one small but powerful fraction of the world is self-centered, the vast majority of the world could be near starvation. When one part of the world chooses to exploit and exhaust the resources of the earth, the rest of the world and all posterity could go begging. A lack of concern for others can produce suffering.

But God was not content with the results of man's disobedience. He decided to intervene, to do something about it. He intersected history and time with a promise, with a call to faith. Throughout history people have looked for the coming answer, the incarnation of a Deliverer. And those who believed this promise found the peace of God in their hearts.

Finally, God came through the Incarnation of Jesus Christ. Christ became one of us and lived among us. We look at him and say, "How did he deal with the question of evil? What did he do about the suffering in the world?" He did two things. On the one hand, he related to it with a healing hand. He delivered those who were in need. He was compassionate to those who were ill. He reached out. When a little girl died, he raised her. When his friend Lazarus was dead, he called him to life. And when people were ill or blind or lame or paralyzed, it was his hand of love and compassion that gave them strength. He lived in a world of suffering and he knew it. Towers fell on people and killed them. Catastrophes occurred. Jesus walked among us, was one of us.

Along with his compassionate and great heart, through which he reached out to those who suffered and brought them to the health they craved, he submitted to the suffering world. Mysteriously, he bowed before its authority, before its inexorable law. And we see him, the innocent One, suffer. He became the sacrificial victim of the curse of sin. Christ accepted it. And so there is, on the one hand, his healing response. On the other hand, there is his submission, to give us an example of how an innocent person faces suffering.

But did Jesus stamp out suffering? Obviously not. At least, not yet. And we ask, "Why not?" If God, indeed, would deliver man, why did he not do it? If God decided to extend redemption to men, why aren't all men redeemed?"

The world is of God's making, and it is for man's use. And man, at the head of this creation, assumes reponsibility for it. Like nature that functions by natural law, man must function by

natural and moral law. The difference is that nature is locked
into its system, while man has the freedom to deviate. The only
absolute and comprehensive way God could have solved the
problem of the disease of man's body and soul would have been
to lock him into a system as nature is locked into its system.
Or, he might have stayed with us every step of the way, like
a mother stays with a little child to be sure the child does not
fall and skin his knee. One or the other of these alternatives
would be demanded.

But in either case it would obviate the nature of the human
being God created in the first place. He created a person who
is free to choose, responsible for his action, to live in the world
which he could either use properly or abuse.

God chose to honor his creature as a responsible being with
freedom of choice. He chose not to take freedom away from
him. So, his offer of salvation is not received by everyone. The
work that was accomplished by Jesus Christ, though efficient
for everyone, is not, in the final analysis, a satisfying answer to
their need because they do not claim it by faith.

We all live together on earth, those who have responded and
those who have not responded to that healing ministry of
Jesus who came to renew his creation. Some of us think that we
would rather live in a magical world where, when ill, we call
on God and we are instantly healed. Christians would become
well; non-Christians would remain sick. Christians would find
solutions to every need; non-Christians would live in their
misery.

Some people think they would like that kind of world, but I
doubt it. I do not think we would want to live where God
would obviate all the natural laws that govern health and
well-being. If we could violate his rules, and he always would
come to our rescue, it would deny his justice, and our respect for
God would suffer. Most of us would much rather make adult
choices and stand by them, living in a responsible way.

We ask, "What happens when we become the victims of
natural catastrophe, such as, earthquakes, floods, volcanic
eruptions as at Pompeii, and so on?" Is nature in itself evil?
There is nothing wrong with the rules by which it functions.
We are not wise when we decide to live in dangerous places.
Nor are we wise enough to project all of the natural events.

In our weakness we sometimes are caught. Or in our foolishness we get hurt. Flood waters do rise, we know, every so many years. And there are faults in the earth. Yet we persist in living in dangerous places. Then when a catastrophe happens, we say, "Why did God permit it?" That is really not the question. The question, rather, is, "When will human beings learn?" Much of the suffering in this world could be alleviated by following Jesus. His compassion, his sensitivity, his patience, generosity, and wisdom were exemplary. This leads us to the next question: "What has God done about suffering? If he hasn't eradicated it, what has he done?"

In Jesus Christ, he has done at least two things. First, he came into this world and became one of us in our suffering. He experienced what we experience. The very subject that is before us was before him. He suffered through the things of the world. Suffering did not originate with him, but he took it upon himself. Being an innocent person born into this world, he chose to identify to such a degree that he willingly suffered. He was the innocent one, suffering for the guilty. And it is in that very suffering that we find the work of our redemption. Suffering was dealt with through suffering.

Jesus came to be one of us. He was not immune from it, but in the supreme horror of suffering he brought the supreme victory of life. And he also became One to whom we can cry because he understands when we call upon him (Heb. 2:18; 4:15, 16).

Jesus said, "I am the way." He also knows the way of suffering. He was not a rebel. He was not a stoic. He was not an escapist. He faced the world as it was. And when the world did its worst, he could have called down angels to help him. But he said to Peter in the garden, "Put up your sword." He could have performed any miracle in his own behalf. His persecutors said to him on the cross, "If you are the Son of God, save yourself and us."

But Jesus knew that he must go through this suffering to understand the need and the forsakenness of man. And in the loneliness of his darkest hour he cried, "Why hast thou forsaken me?" He was forsaken so that we would not have to be. He had a deep faith in the outcome of the cross. He died the kind of death that was most horrible, the suffering of the innocent.

But that is not the last word. We are told in Scripture not to be afraid for he is with us. We who suffer may remember that he suffered. He wants us to catch a glimpse of the eternity to come which will give us the grace to be a witness that the suffering of this world is nothing to be compared with the glory that will one day be revealed.

So what are we to do about suffering? We ought to ask more questions about man and the nature of his freedom and how he has used it. We should ask questions about man and how his world has been affected by his sin. Then we would ask fewer questions about God who seeks to preserve our character and who offers his redemptive love to everyone who will listen. Then we Christians will know that the suffering we are facing is only for a transitional period. We will also study and plan within the moral context of the nature of man and the functioning laws of nature itself. We will pursue every avenue to arrest the evil and assist the good, to bring healing, to feed the starving, to teach the illiterate, to accept our ecological responsibility.

The Christian, of all people, should understand the redeeming work of Jesus Christ in a world where the innocent are suffering. We will know the heart of God who created his world good and perfect and who, in his love, preserves our nature so that we, too, can love. No robot loves, for only a free person can. God has preserved that capacity, and in so doing, he has preserved the potential for suffering. But when our perspective is right, we realize the one far outweighs the other.

Why do the innocent suffer? Why did innocent Jesus suffer? Why did he stand so solidly in suffering? Is it in the innate goodness of man that will support us and answer our questions? Or is it, rather, the graciousness of the condescending Incarnate God which reaches us? The real question is, "When will man realize his potential of living in harmony with the creation and its Creator?"

Suffering Constructively

Suffering often affects people other than the ones in pain. It hurts to see those we love going through suffering. Sometimes when we are the ones in pain, the way our loved ones respond to our suffering tends to add to our burden and causes alienation as we then seek to hide our agony from them. Loved ones sometimes withdraw from us in weakness, leaving us lonely, simply because they can't bear to see us in unfortunate circumstances.

Those who suffer have a certain responsibility to others to bear the difficulty graciously and with understanding. God has not left us without instruction and guidance in this important matter. It is essential for all Christians to learn how to turn suffering into the greatest amount of blessings for ourselves and for those who witness our times of affliction.

In this regard Job is a man worth knowing and understanding. He was at one time a very prosperous person. His business went well, and he had accumulated a great fortune. He also was blessed with a fine marriage and ten children, seven sons and three daughters. He was healthy also. So it appeared that he had everything—all the opportunities in the world with a life filled with prosperity and joy. He was also an upright man, one who served God. Satan, however, came to God and said, "Why shouldn't he, when you pay him so well? . . . But just take away his wealth and you'll see him curse you to your face!" (Job 1:9-11, TLB).

The Lord replied, "You may do anything you like with his wealth, but don't harm him physically" (1:12, 13, TLB).

And so one day a servant came to Job and said, "Your oxen were plowing with the donkeys feeding beside them, when the Sabeans raided us, drove away the animals and killed all the farmhands except me" (1:14, 15, TLB).

He had no sooner gone when another person came and reported that there had been a great storm and "the fire of God" fell (probably lightning) and destroyed his seven thousand sheep and all his shepherds (1:16).

Then a third servant came and said, "Three bands of Chaldeans have driven off your camels and killed your servants, and I alone have escaped to tell you" (1:17, TLB). All Job's assets were gone. His business had collapsed.

And the devil decided to strike again. This time it was his family. His seven sons and three daughters were all partying when a tornado struck. The house collapsed, and all of his children were killed. Job's wife, thinking about their losses and their loneliness, counseled him to curse God and die. What was the good of living if everything they owned was gone? But Job refused to turn his back on God. He still believed that God was in heaven and was caring for him. As he pondered his losses he fell down upon the ground before God. " 'I came naked from my mother's womb,' he said, 'and I shall have nothing when I die. The Lord gave me everything I had, and they were his to take away. Blessed be the name of the Lord' " (1:20, 21, TLB).

Later Satan got God's permission to touch Job's body but he was commanded to spare his life. So Satan caused Job's body to be covered with boils, all over his body and even the soles of his feet. He couldn't stand, sit, or lie down comfortably. There was nothing he could do to find relief. He was in total misery, physically and mentally. He had lost not only his health but his family, and business as well. The devil was certain Job would curse God. But instead Job said, "Shall we receive only pleasant things from the hand of God and never anything unpleasant?" (2:10, TLB). So Job refused to say anything against God. But it is clear that Job didn't understand why the troubles had come upon him.

While Job was in his misery, some of his friends came to sit with him, trying to console him. Job broke the silence, wondering aloud if it would not be better if he were dead. He thought there was no reason for him to exist on earth any longer. At that moment, he could see nothing ahead of him but pain. So his friends began to offer counsel to him.

Eliphaz told Job he was being punished because he was a hypocrite, someone who appeared to be a good and upright man. But deep down, God knew better.

Bildad said he thought the judgment was due to Job's sons, who were not nearly as good as Job was. Judgment on the sons brought punishment to all the household.

Another friend, Zophar, said he thought the reason Job was suffering was due to his lack of compassion for anybody else. Because Job had lived in such luxury, he didn't appreciate what others had suffered. Now it was his turn. He was being taught a lesson, Zophar thought.

Then a fourth friend named Elihu told them not to give Job such a great guilt complex. Although he was young, he hesitated to speak, but he wanted to volunteer something. He thought that Job must be a sinner who ought to repent and confess his sins and get it over with.

But Job insisted on his innocence. "If I have lied and deceived—but God knows that I am innocent—or if I have stepped off God's pathway, or if my heart has lusted for what my eyes have seen, or if I am guilty of any other sin, then let someone else reap the crops I have sown and let all that I have planted be rooted out. . . . Let the Almighty show me that I am wrong; let him approve the indictments made against me" (Job 31:5-8, 35, TLB). Job said these things believing that he would be tested and at last proven true.

Many of us don't have answers to such a dilemma. Some of us think very much like Job's friends. We believe that when people suffer greatly they must have done something very wrong. Goodness means prosperity, and badness means condemnation, poverty, illness, and judgment. But then we recall that many of the wicked prosper and many of the so-called righteous outwardly appear to suffer. It doesn't quite add up. Many of us are in just such a dilemma today. We wonder what we and others have done to deserve such misery and, at the same time, why those who obviously sin do not suffer any more than they do.

Many of us are like the disciples who were asking about the

man who was blind from birth. The disciples came to Jesus and asked, "Why was this man born blind? Was it a result of his own sins or those of his parents?" (John 9:2, TLB). Jesus replied, "Neither." We often try to see the connection of cause and effect. People say, "If you work hard, you get ahead. If you believe in God, he blesses you materially." Many are not willing to accept the fact that one can believe in God, be utterly sincere in his dedication to him, and still have to suffer. We are tempted to seek a correlation. Some feel very guilty when they suffer losses because they think they must have done something to provoke it.

Perhaps such people have what C. S. Lewis called "a grandfather notion of God." We believe that God ought always to be kind and good. And when misery and suffering occur in the world, we think he is absent or that he is powerless. We wonder what happened. We like to finish every single day saying, "And a good time was had by all because God was there." When a good time was not had by all, we wonder where God was and feel that God is perhaps capricious.

There seems to be no sense as to why some suffer and others do not. It is as though God is playing a dart game. He throws his darts at the world, and they hit one person and they miss another. Or perhaps his dart hits India, and a whole nation suffers from poverty and famine. We don't know why. There seems to be no justice and no reason. Our only conclusion is that luck or chance controls the world, that God somehow plays a very remote role, if any, in the suffering of humanity.

On the faraway other side of the ledger, there are those who are Christians, Bible students, that say, "Oh, the suffering of the world is from God. You ought to thank him and praise him for everything. Be thankful for suffering." Rejoicing over pain was not the way Job dealt with it, nor does it seem logical for us to deal with it that way. Why should one go to a doctor to get well if he is going to praise God because he is sick? We cannot logically have it both ways. If suffering is bad, then we try to overcome it. If illness is abnormal, we want to become normal again. If God's world was not in the beginning intended to make us suffer, then we must fight suffering and we must be compassionate toward those who hurt. I do not think we ought to praise God for evil in the world.

Jesus didn't. Remember what he said in Gethsemane? "Thank you, Father, for the coming trials?" No! He said, "Father, if you are willing, please take this cup of horror from me" (Luke 22:42, TLB). And he sweated as it were great drops of blood. He was not anxious for that kind of suffering at all. But he was willing to accept it because he understood the reason for it.

I think we use the wrong preposition when we say, "Be thankful *for* everything." We should say, "Be thankful *in spite of* some things. Always give thanks to God while you live and breathe." We do not counsel with a man like Job and say, "Job, be thankful for what has happened to you." With patience, respect, humility, and wonder, we praise God in the midst of problems, but not *for* them.

When we suffer it is natural that we want to know why. In this we are like Job. He wanted God to speak to him, knowing that God must have had a hand in what was happening to him and he simply wanted to know why it was happening.

Job was like the disciples of Jesus who, confronted by the man blind from birth, asked, "Who sinned?" On another occasion, as Jesus was discussing sin and judgment, he reminded the people of a recent tragedy. " 'What about the eighteen men who died when the Tower of Siloam fell on them? Were they worse sinners than other men from Galilee?' he asked. 'Is that why they suffered? Not at all!' " (Luke 13:2, 3, TLB).

It was not necessarily due to specific sins that God judged them. Who knows what happened to the tower of Siloam? Perhaps they did not build it with good mortar. We do not know. We cannot say that God specifically singled out these people for the tower to fall on.

But we would like for God to tell us what he is doing in our lives. We try to bring him into account, to call him into our court. We say, "Now, God, you account to me. Why are you doing this?" If he does not tell us why, we either assign him to the remote reaches of the universe, or we say he does not exist. Job refused to do that. He was simply puzzled, and he wanted God to tell him why he had permitted the suffering to come.

At times when something goes wrong, we are tempted to justify ourselves, which means we are accusing someone else — often God, for the evil. Job wondered, but was not quite willing to make the accusation. "How could these things happen to me?" he questioned. "What is there, God, that I ought to understand from it? Can I use this suffering constructively?"

But God came to Job and said, "I am going to demand some answers from you. . . . Where were you when I laid the foundations of the earth?" (Job 38:3). Where was Job when God created the stars and when he placed Pleiades in the heavens? Where was he when God created the hawk, the crocodile, and leviathan in the depths of the sea? Where was he when God fashioned the snowflakes? Did Job understand all that? Was Job able to stand in God's presence as an equal and say to him, "Give me an account of suffering?" Is that what Job was saying?

Job was humbled and had to admit he did not know how God did these things in the world. How could he understand the mysteries of how the universe has been fashioned? All he knew was that the great God had done it, and that he could trust in God as his guide and his friend. God was saying, in effect, "Then do not call me into account as though you have to know my mind. You have never understood my mind. Why do you think you need all of the details now?"

Fedor Dostoevski, famous Russian novelist of the last century, struggled with the sufferings of the peasants of Russia, the slaughters that had gone on, the godlessness in the world, the great power wielded by the ungodly over the godly. The conclusion to which he came was that among humans there is no such thing as pure innocence and absolute guilt. That kind of relationship, he claimed, exists only between God and man, not between human beings.

The suffering in the world comes to us all. Not one is sinless. There is none that can plead innocence. God explained to Job that the world was created good. The evil was what man had done to it. The record is very clear in Genesis 3 as to what has happened in our world. Suffering and misery came because of Adam and Eve's rebellion and rejection of the Almighty. When we rule God out, it is not surprising that we suffer, and like Job, we are humbled in God's presence.

Job was being told not only "Why should I account to you?" but also, "What if I did give you an explanation? What good would it do you? It would not be constructive." God did not tell Job about the initial conversation with Satan. He said, in effect, "Job, it makes no difference whether or not you have an answer to the question. The difference lies in your attitude toward me. Do you trust me? Am I really God to you? Or, do you have some misgivings which prompt you to look at me as though I must pass your examination before you are willing to put your confidence in me?" Job was reminded of the character of God himself.

The alternative to trusting God is to reject him in anger and bitterness and to look at this world as though it is not dealing fairly with us. When we turn against God and we see nothing but a capricious, evil universe, then we have nothing to hope for and the future is then anything but bright.

But we live on the other side of Calvary and Easter. Jesus said that, in spite of the garden where he wrestled over his coming suffering, he was willing to say, "Not my will but yours be done," because he had enough faith to believe that his Father worked all things together for good. If we lost our wealth and our family and health, could we still believe it? Could we say, "When he has tried me, I shall come forth as gold"? (Job 23:10, RSV).

This remarkable man Job, does something that displays his integrity and faith. He bends his knee and prays for his friends, asking God to enlighten these men and show them the truth so that they are not always looking for all of the details and the answers of life as though good and bad can always be separated as wheat and the tares that grow together. Job is a man worth remembering, for when you and I are tested and tried by God's prescription, he demonstrated how we can come forth as gold.

Handling Grief

As a pastor and friend, I have been walking in the shadows of grief with people for thirty years. We have trudged to gravesides in all kinds of weather, laying to rest the earthly remains of the elderly, of the newborn baby, of spouses dying an untimely death, and of parents. I have stood with some who mourn a loss caused by suicide. To share with those who suffer the tragedies of lost relationships is part of a minister's duty. It becomes a privilege. I must confess that it became far more meaningful when I stood by the grave of my own mother and then my father, and finally my sister-in-law who, in an untimely death, left my brother and his three children.

A man named Ezekiel, who lived in ancient times, was instructed by God to deal with grief in a very unique way. We do not know much about the man, but we do know that he was one of the exiles who lived over a hundred miles up the Kama River from Babylon. Nebuchadnezzar had conquered Judea and carried off a number of the people as slaves. Ezekiel, living in far off Babylonian territory, remembered with his people the wonderful temple in Jerusalem, the beautiful place of worship, and the former power of a people now subdued to slavery. In all of the events of his life, Ezekiel learned to demonstrate the presence of God.

On one occasion God came to him and said, "I am about to take the delight of your eyes [your wife] away from you at a stroke;

yet you shall not mourn or weep nor shall your tears run down. Sigh, but not aloud; make no mourning for the dead. Bind on your turban, and put your shoes on your feet; do not cover your lips, nor eat the bread of mourners" (Ezek. 24:15-17, RSV). And so, Ezekiel was obedient; he did not disclose his grief.

The question is not, "What did this unusual response mean?" but rather, "Is this a normative way to deal with grief?" Some Christian people feel that because they are Christians, they shouldn't grieve, but must hide their feelings. To them it is a sign of weakness and a lack of faith to grieve over the loss of a loved one.

Wouldn't it be wonderful if we could eliminate grief altogether? We talk about getting rid of worry, anger, fear, and guilt. Why not get rid of this emotion of grief? Is this possible?

All of us, at one time or another, are numbed by loss. Our turn will come if it has not already. To eliminate grief, we would also have to eradicate love. To love is to make a commitment by which our lives become intertwined with another person's life. When death parts us we are left with grief. Some people are afraid to love because sometime in the past they have been hurt. To avoid the hurt again, they resist ever giving themselves to another. They attempt to go through life without ever loving with total commitment. Love cannot be real if there are reservations. Is it not better to love and risk the loss that death may bring? Is it not better to love rather than live in isolation and in fear, and loneliness? We cannot eliminate grief unless we are willing to pay the price of eliminating love.

Nor can we eliminate grief unless we can halt change in the world. Some of us do not like change, because it threatens us. When someone close to us is removed, our whole world is suddenly different. We wake up in the morning and the sun is a little more pale, and the things we thought were important are no longer important at all. Everything has an eerie, phony look. With many areas of our lives we become totally disinterested. The change calls us back to our childhood sense of insecurity, and we no longer dare use anything, administer anything, or touch anything with any sense of finality. It suddenly occurs to us with devastating impact that we are creatures of time. We are mortal, and things about us will eventually pass away. We cannot escape change any more than we can live without love. Grief is for the human being, and it comes to every heart, to every life. It enters every family, and it speaks with finality.

How do we grieve? Wayne Oates, in his book *Anxiety in the Christian Experience* (Waco, TX: Word, 1971), talks about the six stages of grief we all go through. Some stages are very brief. Some of us hasten through the stages while others take more time. But if we understand what those who are grieving are going through, if we are prepared to go through the cycle ourselves, we can handle grief better, and be of more help to others in their own grief.

The first stage that comes is the shock of what has happened. Somewhere in our subconscious we react — some people emotionally and physically, perhaps by fainting. Others react mechanically as they handle the arrangements that must be immediately made in calling doctors, hospitals, funeral directors, and relatives. Whatever the reaction, it is a mechanistic response, not done with deep study or intent. In a few hours this stage is over, and then the frozen feelings emerge. When the crisis comes we were numbed by what happened — like the person who had Novocaine in his jaw and knows the tooth has been removed, but cannot yet feel it. In that kind of numbness we become busy with the arrangements. We sometimes go to a funeral and say, "Doesn't he or she handle this beautifully?" The fact is that they are still numb from the loss and are not yet aware of what has really happened. And then it strikes them as the second stage begins.

The third stage is the struggle that goes on in one's mind between reality and fantasy. We wonder, "Did it really happen? Is he really gone? Can I not talk to her anymore?" An inner problem arises, the unreality of it all. We subconsciously listen for the familiar step on the walk, or wait for the phone to ring when the person will be on the other end and in the customary fashion say, "Hi there." And then we pull ourselves together and say, "It is not going to happen."

Abraham Lincoln went through this stage. During the Civil War with all of its burdens, he lived in Washington with his two young sons, William and Thomas, who romped around the White House. When he would come back from his heavy responsibilities of the war, they would be there to lighten the atmosphere for him. But then in February of 1862 Willie died, and Lincoln, like Ezekiel, had to steel himself and go on with the affairs of the nation.

On one occasion Lincoln was at Fort Monroe on a warship when he picked up and read the passage in Shakespeare's *King John* in which Constance was thinking about the loss of her son. When he was reading through it, he turned to his aide and said, "Did you ever dream of a lost friend and feel that you were holding sweet communion with that friend and yet have a sad consciousness that it was not at all real? Just so I dream of my son." And then this great man put his head in his arms on his desk and in uncontrolled sobs poured out the hurt that was in his soul as he struggled between the reality of what had happened and the fantasy of what he wanted to believe.

Once we reach this stage, our emotions can emerge — all the resentment, anger, sorrow, and tears. We relive the past and good times, and our system is cleansed. We begin to open ourselves to healing. But it is a private healing. There is another step that follows. It is the step of painful reminders of what went on in the life of this dear one. Emotions erupt, sometimes even with physical problems.

Dr. Granger Westberg has written a booklet entitled *Good Grief.* In it he relates how he told his nurses that probably 10 percent of the people in the hospital were there because of some major grief in their lives during the past months. The nurses conducted their own survey in the wing of the hospital. They discovered that it was not 10 percent but 38 percent! While some of it may be coincidental, that is too high a percentage to say that it is *all* coincidental. The grief that finally emerges takes hold of us physically, too, and at times we must pay the price.

Then there are experiences which remind us of the past — anniversaries, the first holidays, and all the beautiful remembrances we have. As they encroach upon us, we feel lonely and have a longing for the former times. Then, later, there breaks upon us, like a new day, the affirmation that the loss is real but that times belong to God. The day will dawn once again, and we refuse to grieve in hopelessness. We accept our humanness for what it is. We had, and we have lost. We had invested, and it is gone. And as the Psalmist cried: "Weeping may endure for a night, but joy cometh in the morning" (30:5).

A minister friend of mine lost his wife at a very young age. He had to be both mother and father to his two little daughters. He said, "You know, Art, after a certain amount of time, you turn a corner and life begins all over again, and you begin to handle your problems."

Ezekiel's wrestling with his problem was not normative. For him, it meant to keep face with the people. He had a message to bring. He had to be strong and unemotional. For Jesus, it meant total weeping at the loss of Lazarus, his friend. Everyone could hear him. Everyone could see him; he is our Brother and he, too, had to handle his grief.

Two things should be said about handling grief. First, we have a God who understands what we are going through because he went through it. With his beloved Son on a cross crying, "Father, why have you forsaken me?" he let his beloved Son die. Ours is a God of the nail-pierced hands. He is One who understands what it means to sustain a loss because of love. But he takes that loss, and he cleanses it of all its bitterness. And as time passes, great blessings come from the loss that can be offered to the world. Because he was willing that his Son should die, we can now offer healing to men and nations. God understands and he comes to us anew in Jesus Christ that out of our grief can come deepening of character and blessings for another day that we do not now understand.

Second, we need to remember that Jesus said, "Let not your heart be troubled: ye believe in God, believe also in me. . . . I go to prepare a place." Do you know where your loved ones are? Your loss is their gain. Christ is there. He is preparing like those who prepare for the coming of a newborn infant. So in heaven a place is made ready. Although the hurt is deep below, we can understand that Jesus is holding out to us his personal word of comfort not to be afraid, for he will be there waiting. And what is more, we will meet our loved ones again.

The Christian, then, handles his grief, real as it is, stage by stage. Although we must plod through the experience, nonetheless we handle it with a hope and overarching possibility — no, a reality — that one day we will meet when all things will become new in Christ Jesus, our Lord. That is our hope. We can give it away to everyone who is seeking to handle grief.

For the prophet Ezekiel, the death of his wife was a critical experience. Here was a man living a long way from home as a captive in Mesopotamia. He and his fellow countrymen were taken there by force. They left behind a beautiful city, David's Jerusalem, with its magnificent temple. And they held in their mind's eye a picture of that citadel which was unfaltering in its strength. It nurtured within every exile a faith and a hope that continued to strengthen them on their pilgrimage in this distant land.

While Jeremiah was telling the people in the city of Jerusalem of their coming doom, it was the task of Ezekiel to destroy the illusion of these captive people that Jerusalem was an impregnable city. The city would fall. The temple would be destroyed. All that these people held in their mind as something upon which they could depend was about to collapse. The love of their hearts, the source of their dedication, had to go.

Ezekiel did not bring a popular message. It was a lonely task to be a prophet in Babylon. And then the word came that his loneliness was to be multiplied and intensified by the loss of his wife. When he would lose his wife, whom the Lord recognized as the delight of his soul, he was not to appear to grieve. He was to keep his hat on, his shoes on, and disregard all the mourning customs among his people. This would be so strange to these people that they would react by asking him, "Why aren't you grieving?"

Then he would tell them that they, too, were going to suffer a major loss. They should have the courage not to lose heart, not to question God, but to understand and to steel themselves against the crushing blow that might otherwise have undermined their hopes.

Great hope can also reside within our hearts as well as the hearts of these people. We must in the first place admit to grief. We must face up to the loss and then face up to our guilt. If we feel there are things that should have been done that we did not do, if the person who has left us so unexpectedly did not hear us say what we should have said, we are typical. Not one of us has said and done everything we should have, and we have done many things that we shouldn't have. We could go through our lives with a great burden over our hearts and great emotional distraction if it were not for the fact that Jesus Christ is the One who in both dimensions of life, here and there, forgives and heals. We can tell it to him.

We can face up to the guilt and all of the shame. We need not to
suppress it and sublimate it so that it can rise later to haunt us.
We can face guilt and grief and be through with it.

We must deal with resentment. A thought runs through many
a mind at a time of great sorrow: "Why me? Why did this happen
to my young son? Look at all the other sons. They are healthy.
Why in my marriage? Look at all the other beautiful marriages." By
comparison we feel cheated, believing we have been chosen to
have this heavy burden laid upon us. Why? If anyone could have
asked that question, it was Ezekiel, a man of God. With undying
courage he stood for his Lord, lonely in a distant land, speaking an
unpopular message. And on top of it all, his wife was taken from
him.

We need to ask this question if we have any such resentment
in our soul. "Why me?" is based on the false premise that God is
somehow accountable to us, that the world owes us something.
Until we face up to the resentment, we will not face up to the facts
either. We will continue to ask without really wanting the
answer because we understand that, once we hear the answer, it
will undermine our resentment. And some of us, unfortunately,
like to feel sorry for ourselves. We find consolation in repeating
over and over again those long-gone experiences, looking for
sympathy from others, who get very tired of hearing the story. We
do not want the resentment removed because we love to harbor
something that seems to justify our hurts nurtured in our souls.
We must get that resentment out of our systems once and for all.

Once having faced up to some of these things, I suggest that we
think about a few other things. The balance between the
intellect and the emotions is extremely delicate and difficult to
practice. Grief, being an emotion, can destroy us if it is not
tempered with the intellect. It is rather striking how much the
mind has to do with our Christian practices. (See Romans 12:1.)
On the other hand, to be entirely analytical and intellectual is
scarcely to be human. To expect of everyone what was
expected of Ezekiel is too much to ask, and God does not ask it.

But yet there are things we should think about grief in advance
so that we can be prepared. When I was twenty-eight years old,
my mother passed away. The healthier of my parents was
suddenly gone. I began to cast about for comfort in my first
experience with grief. I searched the Scriptures. I talked with my

most intimate friends who understood and whom I trusted. It was helpful. When we consider our grief in terms of death and the destiny of our loved ones, it will occur to us that there are many beautiful memories that will live on. We will discover a great deal of positive influence of the departed and all kinds of things that we can build upon.

But that is not enough, for all that influence and all of those activities will also one day be lost in the passing of time. Thank God there is more — not cold immortality but the continuity of life. When we ponder the continuing awareness and the self-identity of that person, there is the awareness of who that person was and is, and that intercession is being offered now in the presence of God for loved ones here below, including you and me.

We understand intellectually that we must face the future. There are only two ways; with anxiety or with hope. Both project a future which does not yet exist — fear or optimism. In the one case, our emotions set us on edge because of what we know is going to be difficult and unpleasant. On the other hand, our emotions set us anticipating a better and glorious future. In Christ Jesus, we choose hope. Somehow or other we have to know, with Ezekiel, that God is for us. In Chapter 36 God said, "I am for you" (36:9). While his wife was growing cold in the grave and Jerusalem was tottering and the temple falling, God was for them. Despite the circumstances Ezekiel was bringing a message of hope and encouragement.

We are a step beyond Ezekiel for we have a New Testament. We have another covenant. We have a great seal, a great sign of the grace and love of God. It is magnified a thousand times on Easter morning as we think of the resurrection that conquered death. In the midst of our grief as we ponder the hope that is before us, our sad moments are overshadowed.

To the captives and the exiles of Israel, Ezekiel said, "Of course, we are in grief. Of course, I understand my partner is gone. I will be lonelier than I have ever been in many respects. But I have good news. God is for us even now. Believe it."

With that kind of balance of emotion and intellect, that kind of understanding of what is going on in the midst of grief, there are a few things we ought to do. First we ought to read the Scriptures. From my personal experience with grief and with many others, I have come to the conclusion that there is not much I can say in a time of deep sorrow. What really speaks is the Bible. I believe we need a mass infusion of it. It is something like being treated with penicillin. The first dose is usually a big one. Once we are on the medication smaller doses will maintain a proper blood level until the disease is cured. But to get started, we ought to begin with a good dosage of Scripture.

Norman Vincent Peale tells a story about a mother who heard that her daughter had been thrown from a horse. She went up to a little New England inn at the time she received the initial call, and then she learned the news that her daughter had been killed. Back in the room that night she was pacing the floor in hopelessness when she spotted on the dresser a Gideon Bible. She picked it up and began to read the Psalms. You know how they start, "He shall be planted like a tree, by the rivers of water." She read through and came to that beautiful statement, "He maketh me to lie down in green pastures."

As the night came on and it grew cold in that little inn, she pulled the quilt off the bed and wrapped it around herself and sat in the chair and kept reading. "The Lord is my light and my salvation, whom should I fear? . . . Teach us to number our days that we may set our hearts upon wisdom. . . . He shall give his angels charge over thee." And, finally, the last verse of them all, "Let everything that hath breath praise the Lord. Praise ye the Lord."

And she closed the volume and said later, "You know, when I entered that room, I wanted to die. But after I had read the Psalms with all their beauty and heart and hope, I wanted to live."

The Scriptures are filled with new insights for those in grief, especially from 2 Corinthians 4 and 5 and John 14. We ought to spend time with that great Book—just in quiet time, alone.

Secondly, we ought to pray. I do not mean praying in such a way that we simply tell God to help us. We ought to pray with frankness and honesty like Jeremiah prayed. We ought to pray like Martha spoke to Jesus, who did not think he came on time when she called him, and she told him so. I get the idea sometimes that we treat God like we treat the boss. We do not dare to tell him how we really feel about things. When he asks a question, we say everything is fine. But when we talk to someone else about our work, it is not good at all. Sometimes in the midst of grief we Christians do not like what has happened, but we do not tell God. We only tell him that we love him. That is not exactly honest, is it?

Jeremiah went to God very frankly and said, "God, I am troubled. I do not understand you. Please, if there is any meaning in this, let me know about it. I need the reassurance of your presence. I am getting lost with all of this. I do not like it. It is grievous to me; it hurts." When we do this, the Lord will be our Friend. He will draw close to us, will reach and heal our breaking hearts because suddenly he will speak to us through that Word that we have been reading. Prayer and the Scriptures go together. God will become more real, more meaningful, and we will find that we have a Friend with us. He waits to heal.

Thirdly, we must take those lonely hours and do something constructive for someone else. When we find ourselves drifting away in self-pity, or when we are tempted to spend our time in lonely despair, we must get out of the chair and use our talents—to bake, or sew, or visit a hospital room, or write a letter, or buy a hamburger for a poor man, or assist someone else to get through a problem, or work out a difficulty. There are hundreds and thousands of needs at our doorstep. It only takes the courage and the will to move out and do something for others. Notice, it does not help as much to do something for ourselves and busy ourselves in some hobby or other. What we need to do is to reach out to another person, for the ache is in relationships. We will find the return on what we give is immeasurable.

Dr. Weatherhead of City Temple tells how he mentioned to a man that he missed his wife. The man replied, "Yes, since our boy was killed, my wife has quit reading the Bible and does not come to church. In fact, I cannot get her out at all anymore. The blow was too much for her. She seems not to be able to face things."

What a contrast to the story that E. Stanley Jones tells of the sixty-two-year-old widow in Australia. She received word that her two daughters, missionaries in China, were killed in a riot. She sold everything she had and went to China to take up their work. Since her daughters could no longer do so, she spent herself until the age of eighty-two determined to give herself to demonstrate the love of Christ, even where there was this kind of brutality and devilishness. When she died, she was honored with a remarkable funeral by the townspeople as they laid her to rest next to her daughters.

What contrasts in the way we meet our grief! Remember Ezekiel. As he walked and talked to God and hoped in him, he could stand his grief because he focused on his duties to the people. God told him in the morning his wife would die. But that day he was out ministering to people. He came home at night, and in the evening she passed on. I wonder what he thought when he left her that morning.

Ezekiel was a great man, wasn't he? His faith shames us, for I must admit I really do not think I could do that. But you and I can reach for it. We can seek to do the things we can do and face up to the things that need to be faced. We can understand the things that will help us. We will be like that old Scottish elder who was dying. His daughter came and opened the Bible for him and started to read. He was in great misery and was struggling, and he said, "No, no, Lassie. The storm is on now. I thatched my house in calm weather." During the stormy weather is not the time to put a roof on the house.

And it is much better if we prepare for grief before it overtakes us. We must face it prepared, trusting, obeying. When grief comes, remember Ezekiel, not only for the wheel in a wheel and the dry bones arising. Remember Ezekiel as the man who was prepared for grief.

What About Death?

Most people who fear death really dread the separation which they know death will bring. Many see it as the end of all human relationships. No one likes good-byes. We postpone them as long as we can, which explains why those who see death as the end of all love relationships are reluctant to talk about it. But it is doubtful if anyone can really appreciate human relationships properly unless he does so in the light of what God's Word says about life and death, physical and spiritual.

My first experience with the death of someone I knew well came while I served during my student days as an interim pastor of a small church in Englewood, New Jersey. I received a call that Mr. Westerveld had died and would I please come right away? It was one of those crisis hours that is not soon forgotten. I remember exactly how I put on my coat. As I walked the block over to their house, I pondered just what I could possibly say to someone who was going through an experience that I had never been through myself. And then the verse came to my mind when Paul said he was "willing rather to be absent from the body, and to be present with the Lord" (2 Cor. 5:8). And I found that it was not my experience that was critical, but the Word of God that spoke to the need.

That was the first time I seriously faced the death of another. The time came when I also faced the possibility of my own death. In 1941, I had been asked by a friend to go to Florida with his

family. We left very early in the morning, were speeding across
northern Indiana on a narrow two-lane road, when suddenly we
hit an ice patch, and started to skid across the road toward the
biggest tree I had ever seen. It was coming at us at an incredible rate
of speed. In an instant I was down on the floor, bracing myself
against the back of the front seat waiting for the impact. Through
my mind for a split-second ran the thought of death, the last
thing I expected on that day. The car lurched when we hit the soft
shoulder. We skidded across to the other side but fortunately did
not turn over. The car came to a halt some distance down the
road. This was the first time I knew what people meant when
they said they were weak in the knees. We were all quiet for a time
as we drove off, more slowly and cautiously, for we knew we had
narrowly missed the possibility of death or serious injury.

Not only the elderly think about death. I find that young
people often talk about death, wondering what it is, and about what
happens when we die. Will we still be conscious—will we
remember anything after we die?

As we consider the subject of death from God's Word, we
should seek to strengthen one another in finding not just
information but a source of comfort as well. Some people are not
willing to discuss dying. They believe it means extinction with
nothing to follow.

Others believe that after death one loses identity and is somehow
gathered into that totality of existence, whatever it may be
called. Man thus loses himself in the great "all" of reality.

And a growing number of people believe with Buddhists and
with Theosophists that one lives on by reincarnation. This life, they
say, is but a prelude to the life to come, and that life will be
rigidly controlled by the way one lives here in this life. In Tibet
when a religious leader dies, there is an immediate secret search
for a child who was born at the same instant, who is then enthroned
as the reincarnation of the expired leader.

Some years ago Annie Bissant decided to make the idea of
reincarnation more real for western society. She went to India
and brought back to England with her a young Indian by the name
of Krishna Merdi. She said, "This is Jesus Christ in another
incarnation." Krishna Merdi accepted it for a time but then
decided that it was not his style of living and reneged.

There is a strong belief in reincarnation today. E. Stanley Jones, for example, visited an Indian village where many were dying of bubonic plague. He asked the Buddhist priest who was the leader of the community, "Isn't there something we can do?"

The Buddhist simply replied, "Nothing can be done. It is a result of their previous karma, so do not be disturbed." Believing they would be reincarnated, the Buddhist saw no reason to be concerned.

The possibility of reincarnation is totally unacceptable to those who believe in the Scripture. We find in such a belief that same kind of deterministic philosophy that is going through so much of modern-day thought. Such theories totally ignore and destroy the concepts of the forgiveness of sin and the loving grace of God. A man does not inexorably die and live again to pay for his past. Someone else has handled it. Forgiveness, not reincarnation, is the hope of personal immortality. Furthermore, our forgiveness and our hope has been documented in the life, death, and resurrection of Jesus.

But people do want to know about death and life hereafter. Even humanists can conceive of it in some form. H. E. Fosdick wrote, for example, "A reasonable person does not build a violin with infinite labor, gathering the materials and shaping the body of it until he can play the composition of the master, and then in a whim of caprice smash it to bits. Yet just this the universe seems to be doing if immortality is false." The shaping and the beauty of man and the potential of nature—are they simply to be destroyed? It is unreasonable to think so.

Others during the ages have argued for immortality. Twenty-three hundred years ago Plato wrote *The Republic,* in which he said that poverty, injustice, and sickness must receive a hearing. Truth must prevail in this life or there is no hope. And, if these calamities are going to prevail, then we are most miserable, for there is no sign that they will not prevail on the other side of the grave. Hence God and immortality must influence us as we seek justice.

Georgia Elliott of Cambridge University said that God, immortality, and duty were the three great prongs upon which human life is built. Immortality has much to do with how we behave and what our values are in this life. We find this thought echoed in the last verse of 1 Corinthians 15. Paul wrote a long chapter about death and the great assurance of victory over death in Christ. And he sums up all of it by saying, "Be therefore steadfast and unmovable." This grand faith in God and belief in immortality will come to light in the way we live our lives. Our works will be established even as we believe.

What we think about death has a daily influence on how we live. Somehow we want to believe in life beyond the grave. Werhner von Braun wrote "Today more than ever our survival depends on spiritual principles. Science has found that nothing can disappear without a trace. Nature does not know extinction. All it knows is transformation. If God applies this fundamental principle to the most minute and insignificant parts of the universe, doesn't it make sense that he applies it also to the masterpiece of his creation, the human soul? I think it does. Everything science has taught me and continues to teach me strengthens my belief in the continuity of our spiritual existence after death. Nothing disappears without a trace." Man seeks to understand his destiny believing that after death there is a real world. And, of course, Christians document this through the Scriptures.

We Christians also like to prepare ourselves, not so much by human reason, but by listening to God. Since we often take upon ourselves the coloration of the thinking of our society, we seek God as we relate to death. If we are not ready to die, we want him to do something to prepare us. We try to operate within the framework of miracles and of demands. Joe Bayly, in his interesting book, *The View from a Hearse* (Elgin, IL: Cook, 1973), talked about how Christians try to avoid facing up to death. Joy Bayly had three sons who died.

A month or so after our five-year-old died of leukemia, a sincere, well-educated Christian told me that our son need not have died if only we had possessed enough faith. "You really believe that?" I asked. "Yes, I do," he replied. "Do you believe it enough to pray that your own child will become sick with leukemia so that you can prove your faith?" After a long silence, he replied, "No, I don't."

The summer after our eighteen-year-old son died, our sixteen-year-old daughter was at a Christian camp. A visiting minister, in the presence of and with the silent acquiescence of the camp director, told this grieving girl,

"Your brother need not have died if your parents had only had faith for his healing. It is not God's will for one to die before the age of sixty."

That is Christianity? Of course not! I have met people who have had experience with it in the church I now pastor. We stood in the front of our sanctuary one Sunday afternoon with a woman who had cancer. The elders of the church prayed with her. And she died. Another woman in this church had cancer and suddenly it cleared out of her lungs and she lived for a time. God gave her additional time. Since then she has also passed on. The past summer a little boy in the church was going to have surgery for something that might have been fatal. A group of us gathered on several different occasions to pray for that boy. Today he is in our Sunday school. God answered positively.

Catherine Marshall's book called *Something More* (Old Tappan, NJ: Revell, 1976), deals with her own struggle with the death of a granddaughter. She had to face up to her own faith. Did she believe or did she not believe? Was her unbelief the reason her granddaughter died? And then she recalled that Jesus said, "Are not two sparrows sold for a farthing? and one of them shall not fall on the ground without your Father" (Matt. 19:29). But the point is that the sparrow falls. God is in everything. And the Word says, "Pray believing." The Father may say, "No" or "Not yet." That is his prerogative. But be sure that God is in it. He was not absent when his own Son died on a cross. It happened, and it was not because Jesus did not believe.

Let us not be disturbed by those so-called Christians who would escalate our guilt. Nor let us be disturbed by those who are outside Christian circles, who would dampen our enthusiasm. The atheist Robert Ingersoll, at the turn of the century, stumped the land against God. He would take out his pocket watch and say, "All right, if there is a God, strike me dead. I will give you sixty seconds." Then he would say, "You see, there is no God." But one day his brother died. He stood by the grave and spoke about a comfort and hope that was poles away from what he had said in the midst of health and security. Bertrand Russell, the agnostic, wrote many books calling Christianity nonsense. But he said in his late hours, "What this world really needs is Christian love."

Let us not be too disturbed. Let us rather turn to the

Scriptures and listen to its documentation of death and the next life. It is a beautiful picture. Death has indeed lost its sting. The grave has lost its victory. Paul wrote, "Now we see through a glass darkly" (1 Cor. 13:12). It is all hazy to us. But then we will be known, and we will know, and we will face with all reality and clarity the presence of the Lord.

Job in the Old Testament raised his head amidst all his suffering and said, "I know that my Redeemer lives, and that he will stand upon the earth at last. And I know that after this body has decayed, this body shall see God!" (Job 19:25, 26, TLB). David said, "Yea, though I walk through the valley of the shadow of death, I will fear no evil: for thou art with me" (Ps. 23:4). And Jesus said, "Let not your hearts be troubled. . . . when I go and prepare a place for you, I will come again and will take you to myself, that where I am you may be also" (John 14:1, 3, RSV). He said to the dying thief, "Today shalt thou be with me in paradise" (Luke 23:43). Jesus prayed for the people around him who did not have that kind of hope. The preacher says, "Dust to dust; ashes to ashes; earth to earth." True enough, but the Christian who dies is "at home with the Lord," a totally new dimension of reality.

Christ came to take away the sting of death. When Jesus talked about going to the bosom of Abraham, and as he talked on the Mount of Transfiguration with Elijah and Moses, Christ documented repeatedly the fact that those who had gone before are alive and that he will one day be there to welcome us into his presence. In Revelation 11 are those beautiful words which have been immortalized by Handel in the *Messiah* : "The kingdoms of this world are become the kingdoms of our Lord, and of his Christ. And he shall reign forever and ever." We shall be there with him.

Such knowledge of the future makes a major difference in our view of death. It makes death seem like falling asleep to awaken to a new dimension of reality. Life after death will be like finding ourselves in a place that completely exceeds our expectation, where the sorrow, selfishness, and the alienations of this life will never enter. And the beauty of the presence of the Lord will be everywhere. In the poetic language of the Bible, they have "no need of the sun, neither of the moon to shine in it, for the glory of God did lighten it, and the Lamb is the light thereof" (Rev. 21:23). Now that makes a difference! We will emerge with a calm, secure feeling when we believe this. All of the crises of life fall into place and all our concerns about lost relationships, and our whole set of values changes.

We hear a great deal today about a changing money market and a sagging economy. Some men's jobs are threatened. People are becoming extremely disturbed and wonder what the future will bring. But what is the relationship between the economics and the spiritual commitments which we have? At best, we will have economic need for a decade or two or three, and it will be gone. Can we take it with us? What difference does it make when we know that beyond this life there is a continuity so that the talents we leave fallow here can be exercised there? The abilities with which we have been blessed here but that are not developed and used can be cultivated there in eternity. Life will go on because life is of one piece. In death only a variation of reality takes place.

The Giver of life and the quality of life are the same on this side and on the other side. And that makes this life meaningful as we build for an eternity in the presence of the same God. And in this light, our attitudes about human relationships find true perspective.

The nature of death then is transitional. The nature of death is to make real a promise and a release. Death brings to the Christian a hope and a purpose. Today we lift our eyes and look on things that are not seen and things that are not temporal. We look to the eternal, and we know that when "our earthly house of this tabernacle were dissolved, we have a building of God, a house not make with hands, eternal in the heavens" (2 Cor. 5:1), and we give thanks in that assurance.

The Experience of Death

Our attitude toward the subject of death and dying reminds me of the seven-year-old who confided in his Sunday school teacher by showing her the letter he had written. It read, "Dear God, I would like to know what it is like to be dying. I only want to know. I don't want to do it. Love Michael."

All of us want to know about dying, but nobody wants to do it. We are interested in what is going to happen when we finally face the last seconds of this life. This mystery was pursued some years ago by a group of university students. They went to Dr. Elizabeth Kubler-Ross with an assignment on life crises. They had chosen to study death. They asked if she, a psychiatrist, would help them explore the subject. She was delighted to do so and thought that a series of interviews with the dying would be helpful. She went to her six-hundred-bed hospital and inquired floor after floor and nursing station after nursing station whether there was anyone dying. No one was said to be dying in the hospital. No nurse and no doctor wanted to refer her for interview with anyone who was dying. She discovered that they were very hesitant to speak about death and wanted to protect the ones who were obviously dying from the very thought.

We are all hesitant to talk about death to people who are in fact dying because very often we do not know what to say. But we must be equipped to deal with that extremity. One wonders how anyone could seriously develop wholesome human relationships without facing the day when one or both parties of the relationship will die.

Early in my ministry eleven-year-old Bobby Frericks passed away. I remember those moments in the early hours of the morning. I knelt by that oxygen tent with Dr. Frericks and a colleague of his as they fought to save this young life. While I was on my knees, I scarcely knew what to say. What does a minister, or anyone, say at a time like that except to cast oneself on the love and grace of God? I have known men to travel great distances across the country to see a dying parent. And then when they arrive, rather than speak to the issue, they say, "Well, Dad, I thought it was about time I came and paid a call." Hedging and avoiding the subject, they are not honest enough to say, "Dad, we both know that life is about over for you. Let's talk about it."

We tend to look upon death as an enemy. Perhaps we are not as afraid of the actual process of death itself as much as of what will happen between the present good health we enjoy and the moment of death. We are afraid of a period of suffering. The actual transition to the next world may look rather attractive and exciting, but the interim period is a different story. But none of us has a choice. How shall we deal with it when it comes to us, when it is our turn? We all know that death is inevitable apart from the intervention of the return of Christ. The young can, and the old must. We know it, yet so often we will not face the inevitability because we are afraid of the painful interim period. We enjoy good health now, and we know we will enjoy the next life. But the uncertainty is about what is in between.

All generations—every race under heaven—the Babylonians, the Indians, those of us who live in Western society and those of the East—all have their beliefs about an afterlife. There *is* going to be another life. Creation laws demand it. There is nothing in this world that is not finally satisfied by the gifts of creation. Everything is born to receive something. There is welling up within the heart of man, philosophers tell us, this undying need to live. And all of the potentials of this life would seem to be abandoned if life were snuffed out like that of an insect. There *is* immortality. We want to believe it. We feel we must believe it. We argue for the indivisibility of the spirit which cannot disintegrate because it cannot be divided.

Some time ago, Dr. Kubler-Ross was headlined in the local

morning newspaper—"EVIDENCE CONVINCES PSYCHIATRIST
THERE IS LIFE AFTER DEATH." Dr. Kubler-Ross recorded that she
interviewed a thousand or more persons who were dying. Some
who had an experience of death, or near death, and then returned
to talk about the experience reported the attraction to leave the
body, for the soul to be released, and to be lifted to other heights
of reality. They talked about someone who appeared to be there
reaching toward them, to help, to invite. None of them felt any pain
or discomfort but only an exhilarating feeling. A universally used
term was that of the beauty of lights in the next world. None of
them really wanted to come back once they started to cross that
invisible line between this life and the next. And yet something
compelled them to return to their bodies and to be residents
once more in this world of ours. "But," says Dr. Kubler-Ross, "my
evidence isn't compiled. It isn't quite time to write about it."
How we want to believe it! How we headline it in our newspapers!
Dr. Raymond Moody, a medical doctor in Georgia, has completed
a research project quite independently of Dr. Kubler-Ross' study.
He has come to the same conclusions, however.

People of the New Testament thought about death and dying, and
they found the answers to their own needs. They handled death
beautifully as Stephen did. Those who crucified Jesus were now
ready to kill him. In fact, the stones were beginning to fall. And
as he was pelted by the angry crowd, he prayed for them. He
demonstrated the calm, cool confidence of a man who believed
in immortality and life after death. He looked heavenward and
committed his soul, as did Jesus, into the hands of his Maker.
Paul, the man who wrote: "For we know that if our earthly house of
this tabernacle were dissolved, we have a building of God, a
house not made with hands, eternal in the heavens" (2 Cor. 5:1).
Paul, as he was about finished with life, cried out "I am now
ready. . . . The time of my departure is at hand" (2 Tim. 4:6).

These were not men who just wrote nice things in the Bible.
They were men who lived what they wrote, men who modeled
their faith for us. They were men whom we can look upon as
being not only preachers but practitioners of the things they said.
And their commitment is where we must finally come if we are to
prove our sincerity and the depth of our own commitments.

There is something about dying that is different from
anything else. We talk about our fellowships, the exchange of our

opinions and views, and sharing times. We have Alcoholics
Anonymous where former alcoholics, who still have the problem
but have overcome its power, help those who have not yet fully
overcome or who are in the process. People who have had certain
illnesses phone to support each other, whether it is those with a
heart condition, people with colostomies, or myasthenia gravis, or
any other of the serious diseases or health problems. We try to
help others by the exchange of experience. But I know of no
societies for the dead. Obviously, people cannot come together
and exchange their views of what it was like to have died in order
to support the living by their consultation. Here is one truth in
the Scriptures which must be accepted purely on faith. It will
remain theory and a faith principle until the day we cross
through that narrow gate for ourselves. Then we will not be able
to return to talk to anyone about it. The only One who ever
lived in history who did this was the "firstborn among many
brethren" (Rom. 8:29), Jesus of Nazareth, our Lord. He came
back from death and told us about it. You and I cannot share such
an experience with each other. We can only study the things
which other people believe. Other experiences we can share with
each other but not in the matter of death. We are all the same
when it comes to dying.

Four things helped and supported the New Testament people.
First, they all believed firmly, solidly in life after death. Paul writes
about it in 2 Corinthians 5, and I am sure Paul knew about the
words of Jesus recorded in John 14. Jesus said, "If it were not so, I
would have told you." He would not have let them believe a
falsehood. He would have stopped the rumor and the error. If this
life is all that there is, Jesus would have spoken to them about it.
He was going to prepare a place for them that "where I am, there
ye may be also" (John 14:2, 3). Once when Jesus was about to
send out his disciples, he said to them, "Fear not them which kill
the body, but are not able to kill the soul" (Matt. 10:28). There is
no way to destroy the soul. It is indestructible. The body? Yes, we
will leave it. But the soul will go on. "He that believeth in me . . .
shall never die" (John 11:25, 26). And to the thief on the cross,
Jesus said, "Today shalt thou be with me in paradise" (Luke
23:43).

Second, the disciples accepted the truth about a level of reality
in the next life when people will be "self" conscious. We will

know who we are and will have a memory of the things that
went on in this life, for without that memory we would lose our
identity. We would not even know Jesus Christ when we meet
him if we had lost our memory. We would have no idea who he is,
what he did, or why. But we will be ourselves in that life.

Paul said, "We are confident, I say, and willing rather to be absent
from the body, and to be present with the Lord" (2 Cor. 5:8).
That is the promise, the assurance, the anticipation. We are going
to knowingly understand our own selves. To leave the body is
the condition of being with the Lord in spirit.

Much is being said today about the nature of man. Experts
who analyze and computerize the cause and effect of man's
nature tell us that if they could analyze enough people, man
would be predictable, since we are only a mass of molecules,
functioning by reactions. We then come to the inevitable
conclusion that when this old body is in the grave and all these
molecules disintegrate, we will cease to exist. If that is true, then
God has no reality. He is spirit. He has no brain, no physical nervous
system. God and the angels have no molecular structure as we
know it. They are pure spirits. But they are "self" conscious. They
have a will. They have knowledge. They develop relationships.
The Scripture talks about the soul, the "you" who puts the
information into the computer and draws upon it. The one who
does the programming is different from the program.

When we shed this earthly tabernacle, this old body, as Paul
described it, we will be at a level of existence and reality which is
"self" conscious, out of the body but with the Lord. Ours will be
a "self" conscious life. Paul believed that to depart to be with
Christ was better than being here in this body (Phil. 1:23). No
wonder he could write so optimistically from that Mamertine
prison, where he watched men being murdered before his very
eyes. You can still see the remains of the prison in Rome today, the
place where so many heads rolled. Blood stains are still visible
in this place where people were killed and their bodies pushed off
into the rushing waterway that carried them on down into the
river and out to sea. Paul knew as he looked through his iron bars
that he was to die there one day. And he wrote to Timothy
saying that he knew it was all coming, but he was ready. He knew
about that next life. He was not only writing about it to the
Philippians and Corinthians but to us.

Third, we are going to meet Christ. The New Testament is replete with the same thoughts as Paul expressed. We read that Christ came from the place to which he has now returned (1 Cor. 15:47). We read also about how Christ passed through the heavens to appear in the presence of God (Mark 16, Luke 24, Acts 1). He is now back in God's presence. When he said, "that you may be where I am," it echoes his prayer "Father, I will that they also, whom thou hast given me be with me where I am" (John 17:24). As he passed through the heavens and reached the presence of God, he wanted us there. Better to live with him than to live without him. Better to be there than here.

Yet we read in the Scriptures that the ultimate bliss will be the day when our bodies are restored. We will be with Christ in the interim. It will be like the period from the time of his death to his resurrection. On that Saturday he committed his soul to his Father. Without his body, he was spiritually alive. He then took up his body again by his own conscious act. When we lose our bodies, we shall be like him in that intermediate period between Good Friday and Easter morning. There we will live in a dimension of reality with all the saints and angels and Christ himself. And Paul said, "It is all right. It is coming to an end, Timothy. But I'm ready and waiting. There is laid up for me a crown of righteousness. It is better to be there than here." He not only thought all of this; he believed it. In his mind's eye, he could see it. For him all the problems of death and dying were only the problems of temporary suffering, and then a new day would come. One day we will have a new body when Christ returns and everyone is raised to life. That is the way we will follow that "firstborn of many brethren," our risen Lord. He went ahead. We will all have our Easter.

Fourth, Paul believed that the dead had certain powers. The New Testament faith is that we will have knowledge at that time. Now we see darkly as in a glass; then it is going to be face to face. With our active spiritual interest in those we leave behind we will pray for them just as Jesus is praying for us in that world of the Spirit. As he prayed in the world of the flesh, so he still prays. What a beautiful thought! Departed Christian loved ones are also praying for us. This thought was isolated by Dr. Scroggie of Scotland when his wife passed away. They had lived together for many years. He finally found comfort in the Scripture's teaching

that she was still praying for him as she knew his needs. Those
who are there have a memory of what is here. They know the needs
of those who are here, and their perfect prayers ascend to God in
their behalf.

Paul adds that we will give an account of our lives on earth.
We will know after death whether we have done good or bad, so
there is remembrance. The things in this life will follow us into
the next. There *is* another life, where we will be conscious, and
where our minds will function clearly.

We get ready for that life as the Scriptures say: "Wherefore we
labour, that, whether present or absent, we may be accepted of
him" (2 Cor. 5:9). Life becomes a continuum — this side and then
the other side. We establish values now that will be valuable
then and we take them with us. The goal of life becomes
crystallized in the relationship we sustain with God through
Christ. Strange how we squeeze the last little bit out of our
materialism, how we get upset when there is going to be a
shortage of something. How we defend our popularity, our
reputation, our fame and fortune! Those things become so
important. But one day that will all be laid to rest. We have come
into the world with nothing; we will go out in our naked
spirituality to face our Creator. Then the emphasis will be different
from what is being lived by some of us today. Writing of changed
and false values, Dr. Temple said, "Somebody got into the shop at
night and changed all the price tags. The things that were
valuable are cheap. The things that have high value are thought
about very little and demand little allegiance of time or money."
So the first thing we should do is to get our values straight.

The second thing we should do is to practice faith in the
other promises of God so that one day, when we meet the crisis of
death, we will have solid convictions. The Word of God in other
areas will have proved valuable, consistently true, and beautifully
dependable. The faithfulness of God who is true to eternity will
buoy us up and give us the strength we need when we face the last
ultimate experience of this world. We become prepared for the
next life by our experiences in this one. And the undocumented,
uncharted future of death will become an optimistic hope.

In the book, *A Man Called Peter,* Peter Marshall was taken out of
the house in an ambulance. He had had a heart attack. He looked
up to Catherine, his wife, as he was leaving and said, "Darling, I

will see you in the morning." It sounded like Paul's exuberance as he wrote, "Jesus Christ . . . hath brought life and immortality to light through the gospel" (2 Tim. 1:10). There is no more doubt and fear, for until our faith is sight, we must live with that hope of dying—the grand experience which will usher us into the presence of Christ.

Relationships that Endure

PART THREE

We must always think of life here on earth as a transient
experience. All human relationships — marriage, parents,
children, and extended families — have a beginning and an
end. As much as we may wish now for them to endure, from
Christ's answer to the Sadducees, marriage relationships do
not appear to continue in the afterlife (Matt. 22:30). We will
all be brothers and sisters in the family of God the Father.

But certain relationships we begin here on earth have no
ending, and these are ones we should most cherish. The
union of Christ and his Bride, the Church, is an eternal bond,
and we have a vital part in it.

Basic to all our relationships is our own identity. Character
traits may change, but individual identity and experience
remain constant.

The bond and seal of eternal relationships, with Christ
and other members of his Body, is love, which Paul said "never
ends" (1 Cor. 13:8, RSV). We love him because he first loved
us (1 John 4:19). And we love one another because love is of
God; and every one that loveth is born of God" (1 John 4:7).

Much of our misery here on earth is because of our failure to
prepare for eternal relationships. We are lonely people
because we don't understand our relationship to Christ and
his Body, the Church. We make relationships poorly because
we don't understand ourselves. We love poorly because we don't
comprehend God's love for us.

God's desire for all of us is unity. Christ prayed for it "that they all may be one; as thou, Father, art in me, and I in thee, that they also may be one in us" (John 17:21). Toward this unity we must direct our energies if life, here or there, is to be meaningful and blessed.

We Are Never Alone

We live in a lonely society, but God never intended for his children to do so. More people are said to be lonely today than in any preceding generation. Twice as many Americans live in single-person households as there were twenty years ago. Over half of the population comes from households of one or two persons. Many people have come to feel like the Psalmist who wrote over and over again in biblical times, "I am desolate and afflicted" (Ps. 25:16). "I am forgotten as a dead man" (Ps. 31:12). "I . . . am as a sparrow alone upon the housetop" (Ps. 102:7).

Loneliness has plagued mankind through the centuries. In fact, only one thing was not good when God made man and placed him in the Garden of Eden. It was that he was alone. God said, "It is not good that the man should be alone; I will make a help meet for him" (Gen. 2:18). It was not enough that man communed with God. Man also needed someone at his own level. There had to be peer fellowship before things were the way God wanted them.

One of the things that makes man so great, far above the animals, is that he can examine his own life, assess it, and evaluate who he is. But therein lies the source of his loneliness, for he then realizes that he is the only person experiencing exactly what he feels, living as he lives, having his track of life to run, and that he will ultimately die alone. No other animal or creature, none other of God's creation is aware of that. Contemplating that fact produces an inner ache unless there is a fellowship, a strengthening bond between us and others and our God.

Loneliness is not experienced by people who are among people who know them, who care about them, who give them security. There is no loneliness for those who are accepted by the group. We all want to be accepted by others and to be part of our community, the place we reside, our schools, our institutions, our places of work. We want to be part of relationships where there is mutual commitment, where we can depend on a friend when there is a need, where we feel needed when someone else has a crisis. There is no loneliness under those circumstances.

Loneliness comes when we are in strange places, where we do not know people, where we do not recognize anything or belong to anyone. Our mobility today produces uncommon loneliness in that respect. Circumstances change and we find ourselves lonely. Someone with whom we have shared our life is suddenly gone. We return in the evening to an empty house. We get up in the morning, and no one else is there.

Or, we become lonely because we are rejected, when someone is no longer interested in us. When the abilities we have to offer are no longer needed. We feel like someone who has been displaced by a machine. Suddenly he must look for a new job because that to which he has given his life is no longer necessary.

We are misunderstood by an age group that is going past us because we do not agree with the direction they are taking. We become lonely when we are guilt-ridden and ashamed because of something we have done or said. We cannot share it; we cannot place it on someone else and walk away cleansed. We bear it all alone.

Many of these have been common experiences through the years. History is replete with examples of loneliness. Many people have written and talked about it, but today we are mass producing it. We seem to have studied to make ourselves lonely. We fret over loneliness, but all the machinery to produce it goes on.

Our Christian faith offers a genuine alternative to loneliness. To understand why our Christianity is so relevant, we must understand how our way of life has changed. Formerly, in this country, we lived in communities. Many of us were born and grew up in the same town, sometimes in the same house. Many of us grew up very near our grandparents. Today that kind of stability is gone. Society has shifted so that we are no longer surrounded by that supportive feeling of the extended family. If we do live in a place for some time, we have sealed our homes against our neighbors. A UCLA coach said recently, "I have wonderful neighbors; I do not know any of them." Neighbors to us are persons who are there. We are mildly friendly with them. We say "hello" and "good-bye." If we need to borrow something, we may borrow it. And we are willing to loan a ladder or a wrench. But outside of that, we are not really friendly in any sense of depth and communication.

We no longer shop at a store where a husband and wife are behind the counter. We shop in huge impersonal centers. Even the corner gas station is not run the way it used to be. I used to think that if we ever had gas rationing, I could at least go to the man where I always buy my gasoline. He might give some consideration to his regular customers. Then it occurred to me that the gas station has changed management about three times in the last year. I do not know the manager because he does not pump my gas any more. I pump my own and line up at the window to pay for it as I leave. People are not serving each other very much on a personal basis anymore.

Our automobiles help isolate us, too, since they are such grand creators of privacy. We can come and go as we want and no one can control us. We prize that. We can say things in our cars that nobody hears. One father calls it his "private therapy" van. He takes his van out so that he can shout and rant and rave at the whole world. Nobody knows about it because he is all alone.

We try to fight this loneliness thing. It is like the airplane experience, the airline friendship, or the "stewardess syndrome," as someone called it. You "love 'em and you leave 'em." We have a very brief relationship as flight attendants exude warm friendliness. But it does not last and it has no depth. It is over the moment we leave the plane.

Some build communes to achieve friendship. People who are hungry to know somebody and experience love and concern drift off to places like Jonestown. One lady said she had been a very stable member of a commune — it lasted a full two and a half years. Everybody in the commune was allowed to keep his automobile so that, if things became rough, he could leave. The back door is always open to run from lasting relationships in the world today.

This reluctance to develop lasting relationships is true even among those who are going out of their way to find friends. Psychologist Richard Farsen has said, "The people who will live successfully in tomorrow's world are those who can accept and enjoy temporary systems — self-destructing communities, hit-and-run intimacy, a few days here, a few months there, but with no real commitment because people will then want to be free."

A young executive said to me not long ago, "I know I will not work in this place very long because I can't afford to. They don't raise me fast enough to keep up with inflation, so I have to move from place to place to get my salary scale moving." We have constructed a society so that young men can no longer work in one place for thirty years. Such transience adds to the misery of loneliness.

But something more profound lies behind much of this loneliness. Back in the days when the Psalmist or Jeremiah and the other prophets wrote, they talked about the idols that people were building and worshiping. In the New Testament times the Romans and Greeks also had their gods. They bowed down to these idols as they defined what their gods demanded.

Jean-Paul Sartre died recently. An editorial in a Chicago paper said, "He embodied all the anarchy and despair of the modern spirit — a man without God, a man who recognized no moral code, the last great apostle of human freedom." Indeed, that is the current, modern definition of freedom — no God. In the old days they at least had idols. Whether they were real or phony, they had gods, but we don't appear to have even that. We have exiled God. And our greatest apostles of modernity are saying to us, "Do as you please. Enjoy your freedom. There is nobody there and nobody cares." When we think that nobody cares, we are lonely. This is becoming a lonely planet because we have no God.

"It is not good that man should be alone." We feel like the forlorn sparrow on a roof top. We are looking about into a universe of nothing, and it does not matter what we do because there is no purpose, no One guiding, no destiny. What would we expect of a generation like this? Socially we have isolated ourselves; morally and spiritually we have exiled God. The bottom line is loneliness.

Obviously, the prognosis is not very promising. To live in this kind of age and not to be lonely is much different than to have lived years ago and not to have been lonely. We have to fight the whole contemporary practice of living and thinking. We have to be willing to stand up and say: "I am not lonely because I know a few things about living that others have forgotten and which the majority of people are struggling to find. I know there is a God, a personal God, who created all things. And he is alive and is interested. He has been involved through his Son. He has penetrated history. This is his world. I am part of it. I do not feel that it is going nowhere. There is hope and purpose. God created us and continues to be interested and involved with us. We are his family—brothers and sisters with everyone in the human race—all bearing his image. We need each other as we need him. While we have each other, we will give ourselves in the interest of each other. We will not accept the concept of love which exploits one another—the 'love 'em and leave 'em' attitude, which is a totally devastating philosophy. It can do nothing but destroy. Loyalties to which I will subscribe will be absolute commitments. I will leave no doors open behind me. I will commit myself and pledge myself, even as God has."

God might have acted in a modern contemporary manner. He could have looked at this little planet and said, "What a mess! Look what they have done to my creation. They are a fighting, cantankerous, selfish people. They are developing the most sophisticated tools, not to help each other but to destroy each other. They live in fear. I did not place them on earth for that. I think I will take the back door out. I will start another movement on Mars and leave those people on earth to themselves."

Why did he not do that? Many people do not understand today why he has not abandoned us. They say that if there is a God, he would not allow this world to go on. Therefore, there is no God. What they do not understand is that his commitments are unconditional. He sent his Son to die for those people on earth because he loved them and is committed to them. He says to you and to me, "Commit yourself unconditionally." When something goes wrong, do not run from it; redeem it. Rebuild it. Refashion it. It is better when you do because the forgiveness and the process of reconciliation make the bonds much stronger. That is the kind of commitment which destroys and devastates loneliness.

Those of us who are fortunate enough to have friends and a

community to surround us with that kind of loyalty are not
lonely. There are moments, periods of loss. We all go through the
human experience of temporary loss, dislocation, and disruption.
But it isn't permanent. More profoundly, we always know that
underneath are the everlasting arms of Almighty God.

All this becomes very real to us through the Church. Many
people think the Church is obsolete because they do not
understand what it is really all about. The Church comes alive
when people realize that the solution to loneliness lies with the
commitments made both to the Creator and to our fellow man. We
cannot find any other place in the world like the Church, for
man needs God and he needs his fellow man. God has structured
his redemptive work in such a fashion that Jesus bequeathed to
us his Church, the living Body of believers, who care for each other,
who get involved with each other, who make commitments to
each other. When the Christian has to move, he still has the
Church. He can go almost anywhere in the world and find
believers, and when he is with a fellow believer for five minutes,
there develops a bond of friendship such as we find in no other
place on earth.

To us who are lonely, we should realize that this world has
helped us become lonely. But God says to us that the Lord opens his
arms and says, "Come to me." This means among other things:
Come to my people in this world. Become involved with them.
Make commitments to them. They will not betray you. They will
stand with you. And when you falter and fail, they will pick you up.
They will forgive you. They will put around you the arms of
concern and love. They will do away with that great wave of
loneliness that is crossing our society and getting into some of
our own hearts.

If we have no thought of the lonely people, we must reach out.
And if we are lonely, we must reach out. Those who are strong and
those who are weak must reach out to one another. There is a
unity of spirit under God which will answer the feelings of
loneliness.

Discovering Who We Are

Our age is difficult to characterize. Trying to appeal to today's conscious or subconscious attitudes has produced some interesting insights. Jim Jordan has become the president of Batten, Barton, Durstine, and Osborne, one of the four top advertising agencies in the country, by creating such slogans as "Ring around the collar," and "I'd rather fight than switch." Jordan assesses our time to be one of selfishness. The "we" has been replaced by the "I." He builds his appealing advertising on that thesis. He said in a press conference recently: "There is a staggering amount of selfishness. If there is a theme . . . it should be not we will overcome, but I will overcome."

Dr. Fred Bloom, a psychiatrist, wrote in the *Yale Review* regarding the problems of marriage. He told about a woman who was going to divorce her husband because he was not helping her grow as a person. Dr. Bloom said this therapeutic conception of marriage would have surprised even Freud. Somehow or other, we seem to expect everything to serve us and our interests.

In *Passages* (New York: Bantam, 1977), Gail Sheehy suggests that renewal comes to those who approve of themselves ethically and morally, regardless of the standards of anyone else. We will make up our own minds. We will do our thing in conjunction with what we believe.

Somerset Maugham probably summarized it well in his book, *Of Human Bondage,* when a man named Cronshaw says, "You will discover as you grow older the inevitable selfishness of humanity." Each is for himself in this world. Today's man is influenced everywhere to seek his own pleasure.

The influences through the media have been so subtle many have hardly noticed how it has affected them, much less how they managed to let it get into their system and minds. We Christians are not totally without involvement in our society or in the thoughts and concepts that bombard us from all quarters.

In an interview not long ago with Dr. Karl Menninger, I asked him what he thought was the major problem of our time. He rummaged about his desk, found a book and handed it to me, and said, "Read this. This is by far the best book that has come out in decades." It is a book called *Psychology as Religion* written by Paul Vitz. I read it and discovered that the major theme of the book is the philosophy of selfism, the deterioration resulting from our selfishness, how it began, and why it has become popular. One of the reasons why we have become selfists in our thinking is because many years ago, according to Dr. Vitz, we began to teach our children that father and mother were not the kind of ideals to whom they should look for guidance. Father and mother ought to dissolve themselves into faceless adulthood whereby they become like computers, collecting information and coordinating experience, and then feeding it to the child as he makes demands.

Dr. Vitz writes, "The basic plot of the transactional analysis morality play is that the poor, defenseless but intrinsically happy, good, and creative child, burdened by the mean old parent, is saved from losing the 'Game of Life' by a self-actualizing information processing computer called the adult." Children are taught to be narcissistic, to look at themselves, to feast upon their own beings. Our generation has been told to turn inward. Now, these children are beginning to participate in society as adults. They themselves are becoming parents, who have inordinate demands made upon them in marriage and family responsibilities.

This is happening today because of our refusal or the incapacity to deal with guilt feelings. We have lost the sense of forgiveness because we have ruled out the atonement. So, by semantic manipulation, we have said there is no such thing as guilt because there are no standards for guilt. Each will look after himself.

Or, another way to look at the problem and its origin, says L. S. Jung in *Dialogue Magazine,* is to recognize that the individual has lost confidence in the institutions of our time — the government, the schools and universities, even the Church. They have become so large and impersonal that if we do not take care of ourselves, nobody else will. And so we will not wait for anyone else to watch out for us — we will do it ourselves. We have great suspicions not only of the performance but of the motives of institutional leaders. We have become self-centered people.

The proposition, "My rights come first," it seems to me, gets a great deal of affirmation in our society. Such a philosophy is directly opposite of the Christian position. Paul wrote: "They themselves measuring themselves by themselves and comparing themselves with themselves are without understanding, without wisdom" (2 Cor. 10:12). It is foolish to measure ourselves by our peer group. The Corinthians were having a problem with this, so Paul had sent them some well-written, well-documented letters of instruction. Then Paul, who was an unimpressive person, visited the Corinthian church. His critics there said, "Are you going to listen to that person? Why, he does not look like anything. He is no dramatic speaker. He doesn't have the appearance of being a leader." They looked at the very things we search for in a leader today. Is the message in the medium, or do we look at the message apart from the medium? Back in Corinth they were asking this question.

Paul said, in effect, "Look, I am unimpressive. I do not come to you with any credentials or with the ability to mesmerize my audience. I just come as I am. But the truth with which I come does not depend upon my abilities. You people judge the truth by what someone else thinks or by comparing understanding with understanding. You who live purely on a horizontal level are without wisdom." Shades of our own political campaigns! We make or we break men by television. We see a product in terms of a package rather than its content and its intrinsic value. Paul faced this problem in his own ministry, so it is nothing new.

Jesus, in teaching people to pray, said the first thing they ought to do was not to look at themselves but to God. "Our Father . . . hallowed be thy name. Thy kingdom come. Thy will be done" (Matt. 6:9, 10). We begin not with ourselves but with God.

The writer of the Proverbs said, "Give me neither poverty nor riches." He implied that he did not need either extreme to meet his basic obligations to God.

Christ said on another occasion, "He that findeth his life shall lose it, and he that loseth his life for my sake shall find it' (Matt. 10:39). That is a direct contradiction of the selfist theories of our time. We must give of ourselves. As Christ was a servant, we must become servants. The follower is not ahead of or beyond the teacher. We follow Jesus, who came as the suffering servant, and who suffered for us even when we rejected him.

The greatest thing in the world is love. What is love but giving, even to enemies—giving when there is need? "Who is my neighbor?" one man asked Jesus. Our neighbor is anyone whom we meet with a need. We give regardless of how we are treated in return.

That does not sound like the proposition, "My rights come first." When Jesus taught us to lose life to gain it, he was not talking about losing this life to gain the next life. The words are the same in the original language, suggesting the kinds of life spoken about are the same. We lose what we have in this life to get something now, which we get both in this dimension of reality and in the next.

When Jesus said "He that loses his life . . ." he was not looking for heroics, someone to do something spectacular in an emergency. He was talking about the consistency of life, day by day, the serving and loving attitude. The greatest of these, love, is to be lived day by day, as Jesus did it. We remember him for it.

Does selfism work? We have been trying it now for many years. What is the score as far as these new theories are concerned?

As far as the family goes, we see nothing but a curve upward in divorce. The national average is 40 percent. The average in this area of Illinois is more than one divorce for every two marriages. The family has been undermined and is disintegrating because partners in marriage are thinking first of themselves. "What will I get from this union?" is the consideration. And, when we do not receive, then we think we ought to go elsewhere to find something that would be a little better. Love is giving, but we seem to have forgotten this.

The one who instituted marriage from the beginning of time gave us a documentary on it in his own life. We have forgotten that also. We see that families are failing. I do not know anyone who is unhappy because of good family life. I know of no mother who has invested herself in her family who regrets the fact she has done so. We always enjoy and take pride in our families. To have our families about us gives strength and security to us.

The love that goes with the family is a microcosm of what we would hope society would become. The individuals who are having problems are usually the ones whose families are breaking. Troubled homes are where we find the aching hearts today. The problem emerges in proportion to the degree that our society has redefined, and thereby destroyed, the concepts of Scripture that make marriage work. Let us be sure we lay the problem at the doorstep of the proper party.

Does ignoring the biblical principles work in consumerism and materialism? No. There is a built-in obsolescence for the person who has everything. And, when he has the first thing, he wants the second. There is always someone who has a better one. Next year's model supersedes.

Can careers survive without scriptural basis? Not entirely. *Cosmopolitan Magazine* combines the successful career with indulgence in immoralities and holds up these kinds of persons as the successful ones, who have found in selfism the answer to life. But where do we find the highest incidence of attendance at psychiatrists' offices? Where do we find the highest rates of suicide, alcoholism, and drugs? Why is there so much unhappiness among those, particularly, who have what others think they want? The selfist attitude defeats itself.

The divine imperative is quite different. The proposition that our rights come first is totally opposed to the scriptural message. First of all, Jesus teaches that we find by losing. We have to lose in order to find. It is a paradox, but it is true. Did we ever lose ourselves to find ourselves? How do we discover the character of someone? If we want to capture his personality, how do we get it? If we have a camera and we want to take a picture of someone and see him as he is, how do we capture him? If we interview a football player on television, is that the true person that we come to know? Or, is it the person who is on the field, the one who, in the crucible of action, is reacting and playing the game? Are not the great photographers of the day those who catch people in an off-guarded moment? We see people as they are, as they lose themselves in something in which they are involved.

That is also where we find ourselves. By private meditation, we can reflect on what we have made of our lives and, hopefully, see a pattern emerge. We will find ourselves as we have lived. And we may become old and still not know all about ourselves—the things we can do and the things we cannot do. And we will be surprised.

Jesus is remembered as much for how he lived as for what he said. In all the letters of Paul, he does not quote Jesus once. But he talked about what Christ did. What Jesus did was to express in his life what he taught and to demonstrate the kind of love that he professed. He lost his life. And he gained in the loss. Do we want to find it? Then we lose it! Like Mother Theresa of Calcutta, or Joan of Arc, or Albert Schweitzer, or the Apostle Paul, or Jesus Christ.

Also, totally contrary to the selfist attitude, the Bible shows us how to save by spending. Some of us may be happy to know that. We do not save by conserving muscles, mind, or memory. We have to spend these things. A body disintegrates when it is not used. So does our love. So does our faith.

Many times, we think we can save things and thereby gain. I had an Old Testament professor once who thought this was so. Some of us in the seminary were riding with him from Grand Rapids to Kalamazoo, Michigan. He had a Buick at the time, and he kept it in second gear. We were about ten miles out of town. Finally, one fellow said to him, "Doctor, why have you left your car in second gear?"

He replied, "Well, I always use the third gear, and I thought I would wear the second gear to make it a little more equal."

Saving in order to conserve is totally ridiculous in many areas of life, but we still try to do it. Spend yourself. When we do, we usually get much more in return. When people join the church, they feel the church ought to serve them, so they sit back and don't spend themselves in service. They wait for others to wait on them. The selfist attitude does not work, for such people get very little out of the Church. Such people often entertain themselves by complaining. But, the people who are active and giving—of their talent, their time and money—are the ones who profit most. They are the ones who think that the Church is alive because they are alive through it.

The same thing happens in government and educational institutions. The same thing happens in our families and marriages.

If we do not give ourselves and spend ourselves, we will never save ourselves, our government, our marriages. They will disintegrate and disappear. Lloyd Douglas demonstrates this in his great book, *The Magnificent Obsession*. In the book a young medical doctor was sick of mind and body. When he finally spent himself for others, he saved himself.

Another thing happens, which is rather incongruous on the surface. We live by dying. Remember the words of the father when the prodigal son came home? "This, my son, was dead, but is alive." His son was not literally dead. He was very much alive in a pigsty. He had gone to a far country to indulge himself. He went to find the good life. But the father said when he returned home, "He has come alive."

Jesus said to Nicodemus, "You must be born again." New life has to be infused in us. So, if we die, we come alive. We die to certain things to come alive to other things.

The greatest demonstration, of course, was Christ himself. He died to live. He said that we, too, must learn about our crosses. The Christian must lose life to live. Would we consider Jesus a success? Or, do we think his death was folly? Do we know of anyone who for the past nineteen hundred years has influenced history more than Jesus? Was he greater on Palm Sunday when they were waving the branches and laying their coats in the path of the donkey than he is today? Six hundred million people in this world confess his name. He has become a great influence for good through those persons who in his name have founded the health care centers of the world and the educational institutions. He has moved those who have taught and built the finest traditions of government in the world, those who respect one another as image-bearers with a dignity of the Divine. Do you think he failed? I think he found life by dying. He said, "You and I can invest ourselves and thereby live."

Do my rights come first? Or, shall I be a servant, one who gives in a self-effacing, Christlike manner?

Unfortunately, in our society families are no longer using the weekends to strengthen their spiritual lives. We Americans are using weekends for everything but what they were originally intended. Someone has said that if you want to become wealthy, hold a forty-eight-hour seminar on Saturday and Sunday. Pick a topic. People will come from everywhere to find out more about new theories for successful living. These forty-eight-hour marathons often successfully assault the Church and the family. They tell others that they need not listen to the Word of God. The proposition is, "My rights come first."

We Christians need to see the issues. We must articulate the contrast and maintain our own disciplines as Christians. We must not have God at the end of our scepter as we sit on our thrones telling him what to do for us. We who profess the faith must realize once again that we find by losing, that we save by spending, and that we live by dying.

Love Makes Life

We have all probably puzzled over the definition of love. We talk a good deal about making love, being in love, and the need for love. In a recent issue of *Psychology Today* there was a full-page ad reading, "How to Win at Love — How to Get the Love You Never Thought You Could." The article said that love is a game. Learning how to use the raw power of our love can act like a magnet to attract the opposite sex. For only $20.90 one can get two books that will tell how to use love, how to manipulate it so that others will be attracted to us, and how to get the attention we have craved for so long.

That kind of love is contemporarily defined by Dr. Ernest Vandenhag who wrote, "Love is a passion. It is the tension between desire and fulfillment. As love becomes fulfilled, it ceases to exist. Love is temporary, irrational, unpredictable, and frenzied."

On the basis of that definition, we could merchandise love, for when that love finally comes into existence, it is there for only a short time. If it is a projection, we could live with it; but once the projection or the desire becomes a reality, then it would be all over. Love would be gone. We would fall out of love. And we would go about seeking another relationship, some new experience.

Psychologists have struggled with the definition of love. Harry Stack Sullivan says that the state of love exists when the satisfaction or security of another person becomes as significant to

one as one's own satisfaction or security. Eric Fromm, probably
the father of the definition of love as far as psychologists go,
differentiates five aspects of love. First, there is brotherly love for
everyone in the human race. Secondly, there is parental love that
specifically centers itself upon children and has its own peculiar
qualities. There is erotic love which is the love we share with
others who, in turn, reciprocate with their love to us. There is
self-love which is self-acceptance and self-esteem. And, finally, there
is godly love which arises from hearts that need to know some
god but is not reflexive love to God's first loving us.

Psychologists Freud, Rogers, Goldenson, and William Glasser
all have defined love in different ways; but their arguments all reach
one interesting conclusion. They agree that love is a great
therapeutic for the psyche and brings to us new dimensions of
reality and experience. It heals our broken souls.

Thus, we Christians turns with interest to see what love is. How
can we understand it? Over one hundred fifty years ago a sermon
was preached in New England by Thomas Chalmers, which
immediately became a classic. It was called "The Expulsive
Power of a New Affection" a message based on 1 John. Chalmers was
far ahead of his time in thinking in terms of motivation and of
love. He said that people are never motivated by telling them what
not to do, by removing from them some aspects of their life, or
by telling them how bad things are. Nature abhors a vacuum. The
positive must move in to replace what is gone. The way to win is
to love.

Chalmers said that God came loving, not condemning. He
came forthrightly to help and to heal, not to tell us what is wrong
with the human race. He said that in like manner we Christians
ought to be aware that love has a dimension which is very positive
and which will lead us to the better life, provided we are willing
to accept the positive responsibilities and fill our lives with what
loving requires of us.

Chalmers distinguished two areas of love—one in which the
object of love is at a distance and another in which the object of
love is finally realized. An example of the first concept is a young
couple looking forward to their marriage with great and eager
anticipation. The second concept is realized by another couple
who is married and living on that level of love which possibly
surpasses any other kind of love that we know in human dimension.

The Scriptures have many things to say about love — the love that we express to each other, either as desires or as realities. Love is considered in the Scriptures in three different ways. The first we might describe as attraction. We love because someone attracts us, a kind of magnetic pole or chemistry at work. Something happens between two people. Perhaps it is because they need each other. Each finds some satisfaction in projecting something that the other person has to offer. Perhaps it is sex gratification. It could also be the security of that person, or the age of that person, or his or her achievements that we are accustomed to and need to support us in life. Whatever it is, there is that attractive dimension of love. We respond to it readily when it comes to us, and it is not difficult to recognize.

The second kind of love is what we might call associated love — love because of association or cooperation. Two persons have the same interests. Each likes to do what the other person does. Such persons meet from time to time, participating in these activities, and begin to talk about common interests. When young couples come to our premarital clinic, a psychological compatibility test is administered. The results show a graph which either runs together or runs apart. When it separates, it signals a red flag; and the young couple ought to talk about the area of concern where their differences are obvious.

Couples involved try to find each other on the basis of common interests. But sometimes as the years go by in marriage, interests tend to separate. After twenty or twenty-five years, people suddenly realize that they have lost each other's interest. They are poles apart, and they did not realize that the kind of cement for a lasting marriage had been gradually crumbling and disintegrating before their eyes.

A book entitled *A Severe Mercy* by Sheldon Vanauken (New York: Harper and Row, 1977) is about his marriage, his love life with Davy, and what they did to secure their marriage. They built what they called a shining barrier, something to keep them from drifting apart in their life. They protected themselves against becoming separated in their interests. As time went by, they built new interests but always together. This dimension of love is very important — to find those who are not only attractive, on the one hand, but with whom we can associate in like interests.

Is this really the dimension of love that we are talking about in

1 John? Is this what is called the love that we ought to practice? In 1 John 5:3, we are commanded to love. We are supposed to love. There is no mention of being attracted to someone or having like interests. The Scriptures say and Jesus told his disciples to love as he was practicing it. Jesus was love in the flesh, for God is love. When they practiced that love, God would be in them, he promised.

This third kind of love the Scriptures describe is a giving love — a love that says, "Whatever I have, I want to share with you, and in your interest I want to make you what God meant you to be." It is a love that takes first things first as far as the other person is concerned.

We can see immediately that this kind of love is not emotional. One does not fall into and then out of this kind of love. It is a love of the will. It is something addressed to our volition. We do it because we make ourselves do it. We order ourselves. Because of Christ, we are motivated to love. We do not wait for attraction or like interests.

Nor is this kind of love a contract arrangement. Some people have an idea that marriage is a contract. It is not! It is a relationship. It is not a fifty-fifty obligation. Christ does not give this command so that we have half of the bargain and the other party gets the other half. There is nothing like this in the love of God. His love is unconditional. We must be as unconditional in our love as he is. It is not a few kind words here and there — some do-gooder's attempt to get God to like him or her. It is not a good deed for the day. It is a way of life which extends itself to help the man, the woman, the child who has a need. If we look at that kind we will all agree that such love is a high ideal which we rarely achieve. Even within marriage it is very difficult to love like that, to ask nothing in return, to simply try to please the partner. If both partners did this, it would make a beautiful relationship. This kind of love ought to be not only the goal; it ought to be the realization of every Christian marriage. That is the love that is referred to in 1 John 4: "If we love one another, God dwells in us."

I recently read about a boy from Harlem who had been taken to summer camp. When he got there, he was into all kinds of mischief. He made trouble for the counselors. Eventually, he realized that he was not really getting the attention he wanted and that actually the counselors were looking out for his welfare, trying to help him, caring about him. When he went back home, he said, "I never experienced such love in my life." We can enjoy the reciprocity of love as it flows in both directions. But perhaps initially it flows only in one direction as we love as Christ taught us to love. How difficult it is to do this as an everyday practice.

Yet this kind of love is all around us. It is being expressed in this country even though the papers do not tell much about it. In the bestseller, *A Walk Across America* (New York: Morrow, 1979), Peter Jenkins told about starting out from New England. When he got to Washington, D.C., *National Geographic* gave him a camera and said, "Take some pictures for us as you walk across the country." Part way through his trip, he stopped and wrote his book.

He said, "The thing that impressed me the most was the love that was shown to me. It did not come from those who were talking about welfare programs because they loved the poor and the needy. It did not come from the people who want to make love and do so publicly. It did not come from those who live in communes. You know who it came from? Just the average Mr. and Mrs. America, building their home with their children, and willing to reach down into a pot that is almost running dry for their own welfare, sharing what little they have. They extended love to me, and all of them confessed that they were, first of all, Christians, followers of Jesus."

That is heartwarming and encouraging. It is love in action. It is the love which cares. It represents God in our midst. God is in us because we love. That love is where the giving all started, the caring, the understanding. That is what motivates us. And it is because of God, who does not get annoyed nor disillusioned with us, no matter what we do—God who does not fall in love with somebody else because he is disenchanted with the way we behave. He is the God who reaches down to us in the midst of all of our problems and never changes. He is always concerned.

He is not the God that some of us know. Ninety-seven percent of Americans confess they believe there is a God. When things happen like the crash of a DC-10, they ask, "Where is God?" They ought to ask, Why don't human beings, to whom God has given a brain and a sense of accountability, put airplanes together properly? Why do people build cities at the foot of mountains that erupt periodically, or in the path of flood waters that periodically cover the countryside, or build homes and buildings on faults where they know an earthquake could destroy them?

Let us not ask the question, Where is God? Let us start asking the question about human beings and human accountability. God's love never stops. When we suffer loss, it is God who gives us the promises of his presence and his resources and his assurance of a life to come. He provides in those conditions, but he leaves us free to be human beings in his image to function freely as we love in the context of freedom. What a different kind of God—one who lives and is concerned!

When John wrote his epistles, the secular world assumed God was apathetic, did not care, or was so far away that he did not know about them. But if he did know anything about it, their description of his attitude was *apathea* (apathy). Epictetus probably gave us the best insight into how to handle life as he thought God handles life when he wrote, "Begin with a torn robe or a broken cup and say, 'I don't care.' Go on to the death of a pet dog or a horse and say, 'I don't care.' And in the end you will be able to stand by the bed of your loved one and see the loved one die and say, 'I don't care.' " That was his philosophy for handling life.

Into that kind of society John came and said, "God is love. He cares; he is concerned." Whether we pay our dues in the church or do a little good thing for a neighbor and think we have earned something or not, he still loves us.

And he loves us like Jesus loved us. God came into the flesh to demonstrate what it is all about. When did Jesus ever want people to serve him? When did he strive for popularity? When did he massage his own ego? When the multitudes followed him, he said to them, in effect, "I know why you are following me—because of miracles. I will not do any more miracles. And what is more, I want you to know that some day you are going to be responsible to the Almighty. What you sow, you are going to reap." And the crowds did not like what they heard and left him. He won no popularity contests. It was his attempt to be honest and forthright and to help the people who came to him.

He does not love us because we are so attractive. He does not love us because we think as he does or have the same goals or have the same interests. Our great virtues do not attract him to us. Rather, he pursues us.

When we are down, he comes to speak to us as he did to the

woman at the well at Sychar. In so many words he said to that poor woman living in adultery that he knew her heartache. He knew what she was seeking. She was not going to find it where she was looking, but he would tell her where to find it. "Drink of me, and I will be to you a wellspring of water from within that you have never had before, and you will never thirst again. I can enrich your life beyond any dimension you have ever dreamed possible." And he offered it freely to this poor, despised woman.

When Peter had denied him, Jesus sought him out to know if Peter still loved him in spite of his denials; in spite of the fact that he deserted him at the crucifixion and was not there to care, to support him.

If we can learn to love like him, not waiting to be attracted, not waiting to have similar ideas and goals, but are simply obedient to the command, the imperative of Christ, then we will have God in us. We will have the God who is afflicted in our afflictions. We will have the God of the Old Testament of whom Isaiah exclaimed, "In his love and in his pity, he redeemed them" (Isa. 63:9). John echoed it when he said that the greatest demonstration was when Christ assumed the responsibility for the sins of those whom he loved and went to the cross. There, in the hellish night in the garden of Gethsemane, when God forsook him and all had fled and he wept in his bitter loneliness, he offered to man paradise. That is love that personifies the God who gave himself for us.

Why do we love? Because God loved. He gave and he gives. The good news is that that kind of love changes people. It will change us. It will make our hearts come alive. We will discover that it is the lover who feels better, acts better, thinks better, responds better to life. The days will be brighter and the future more hopeful. It is the person who is self-centered and who has not learned to give that is most miserable in this world. Love that gives leads to attraction and association. And it supersedes all lesser forms of love.

Jesus says, "Love by giving to the person in need." Who is that person? A rich young man asked Jesus that question one day. Jesus answered with the parable of the Good Samaritan. We are to love everybody, whether we are attracted to them or not. We did not select them — God did. And when he wants someone to cross our paths in life, he puts them there. He gives us the same assignment he has given his Church through the ages: to love. We must become a community of love so that when people come to our doors, our homes, or our churches, or when they meet us individually, they will be overwhelmed by a godly style of life. What an earthshaking, life-changing gift — the gift of love — for if we love one another, God is in us.